TRAVEL & TOURISM
AN INDUSTRY FACILITATOR

Published by:
Lotus Press

TRAVEL & TOURISM
AN INDUSTRY FACILITATOR

A.K. Bhatia

4263/3, Ansari Road,
Darya Ganj, New Delhi-110002

LOTUS PRESS
4263/3, Ansari Road, Darya Ganj, New Delhi-110002
Ph: 32903912, 23280047, E-mail: lotus_press@sify.com

TRAVEL AND TOURISM —AN INDUSTRY FACILITATOR

ISBN : 978-81-8382-248-0

Published by: **Lotus Press**, New Delhi-110 002
Printed at: I.Y.N. Graphics, New Delhi-110 002

ACKNOWLEDGEMENT

At the outset, the author would like to acknowledge the contribution of all those who have in their respective publications used certain terms and tried to explain these to make reading of text more simpler. I have always believed firmly that no published work of a author can be completely his or her own especially if the work happens to relate to subjects like travel and tourism or for that matter other subjects in management, arts and humanities. The authors of all the publications whose names are not printed in this book in spite of the fact they have immensely helped in preparation of the book are in fact the legion who have done the pioneering work. My special thanks are due to them.

I would also like to take this opportunity to express my deep sense of gratitude to several International travel and tourism organizations with special reference to International Air Transport Association and Universal Federation of Travel Agents Association whose various publications have been of immense use in helping me in compiling this publication. I am deeply grateful for their invaluable help.

The author always remains indebted to the readers of his work as they are his prime motivators in encouraging him to undertake the assignment. As far as academic work is concerned, it is the students as also the working professionals who provide this motivation. It is their guest for acquiring.

Knowledge and professional qualifications which has encouraged me to bring out this publication. I shall always remain obliged to the student community as also working professionals in travel and tourism industry for their support.

Last but not the least my special gratitude to my wife Kamla for not only encouraging me to complete the work, but also assisting me in editing the final manuscript for publication.

A.K. Bhatia

May, 2010

DEDICATION

Dedicated to our dear parents who have always helped and supported us whenever we needed them.

To Our Loving ***Father***

Who is not with us physically and to whom we miss each moment of our lives with fond memories, deepest love and affection, greatest pride and honour. Although his physical absence is felt deeply, he is always in our hearts. We continue to seek his blessing and affection.

To Our Loving ***Mother***

Who is with us and continues to give us love, affection and blessings. Her presence is a great source of strength to us all.

We pray to almighty God to bless us with her company for many more years.

CONTENTS

INTRODUCTION

Each year, tourists log in millions of kilometers going to and fro hundreds of thousands of destinations in the world, continents. Each year, more and more people from across the world visit private, public and commercial resources and attractions. Each year, total revenue and operating expenses give a great fillip to the tourism industry worldwide.

The demand for tourism generation is all but overwhelming for the people who try to satisfy it. From the time when the pioneer named Thomas Cook over 170 years ago got an idea to engage a special train to carry the friends of temperance from Leicester to Loughborough in England and back to attend a quarterly delegate meeting with over 200 passengers, today when we have plus 950 million international tourists criss – crossing the world's boundaries, the scope and dimensions of international tourism have seen great changes.

The great strides in technology, responsible for creating world class transportation systems on land, in the air as also on the water surface and recently in space have been responsible for creating a travel demand which at times becomes difficult to manage. As the modern technology shrinks the world and creates an interdependent world community with it's special concerns and needs superimposed upon those of it's unique member nations, it becomes urgent that all countries work together in their own interest and in the collective interest of the planet.

On the other hand, with the increase in the tourism demand there has been constant increase in the tourism supply. The transport systems operating in the form of airlines, railways, coaches, ferry liners evolved over the years are constantly being redesigned taking into consideration market dynamics as also changing requirements of the customers. Modern mass tourism can not exist without comfortable, safe and reasonably priced and easily accessible transportation systems. Almost all the destinations in the world depend a great deal on efficient means of transportation being made available to the tourists travelling within their own country as domestic tourists or oversees as international tourists.

Accommodation constitutes yet another important supply elements. It is a vital and rather fundamental part of tourist supply and an important feature of the total tourist image of a destination. The first hotel in the classical sense, the forerunner of the modern day existing complex unit, is said to have been created in Paris, France in the year 1312 AD. Later similar hotel establishments were established in Italy, Holland, Germany and many other countries in continent Europe. Ever since the range an scope of accommodation has expanded to include international hotels, commercial hotels, residential hotels, resort hotels, airport hotels and many more variations. Yet another form of accommodation in the form of supplementary accommodation also came into existence almost in every country. Supplementary accommodation offer only the basic accommodation with limited services unlike hotels which offer complete services. This type of accommodation is moderately priced.

The subject of travel and tourism has assumed vital importance ever since the mass tourism came into being as a result of evolution of jet–age technology. Several Institutes of training/universities have introduced both under–graduate and post–graduate programmes for those desiring to be serving in the ever expanding industry. These programmes are both contact as well as correspondence. Some of these programmes can also be done on line. In addition, short term as also capsule courses are also available for those who are looking for jobs and also work to support their studies.

Over the years, several publishers both in India and abroad have published books written by authors. These books give the reader a global perspective of travel and tourism industry in its various manifestations. The books also try to cover the structure, nature, organizational set –up, marketing and promotion of global tourist industry, planning and its impacts on various social, economic and cultural aspects on visitors themselves as also the host community.

These publication are useful not only for those pursuing tourism studies but also those working in tourism field. These publications in addition also provide useful information to tourism organizations, transport and hospitality firms, travel agencies, tour operating companies and others engaged in travel and tourism business.

Although the tourism publications referred to above explain the tourism phenomenon in simple and comprehensive manner, yet at time it becomes difficult for the reader to find correct and appropriate meaning of a particular term and are rather a loss. For example while reading a chapter on ' Travel Agency Management 'they come across the term 'affinity group'. Many of the readers who do not have the prior knowledge of the subject will get stuck at that point and will require assistance before proceeding further. Another example could be a term 'carrying capacity 'often used in 'planning and environment 'material. This difficulty is encountered not only by students alone but also by teachers and other professionals.

Like in most industries, travel and tourism is full of terms, acronyms and jargon. Confusion arises when different people use terms to mean different things. Different authors may provide different interpretations. What is therefore important is that the definitions of terms used in various publications will found to be consistent and well defined set which will aid value by encouraging for every reader same terms with same interpretation.

The present publication of travel and tourism terminology contains comprehensive glossary as also acronym used throughout the world highlighting the many different usage among many countries. The glossary provides definitions of travel and tourism terminology. Acronym on the other hand is a word formed from the first (or first few) letters of series of words that are used as an abbreviations to refer to that series of words.

The publication contains over 2500 definitions used throughout the world. It covers all aspects of tourism industry including hospitality, transport as also ancillary services. It also decodes important abbreviations often used in the travel and tourism industry. The entries may vary from one line definitions to 100 word write–up. This edition is unique in that it contains cross referencing system, for example accessing any entry about ' business travel 'leads to over 15 others.

The publication is an essential reference tool for anyone involved in tourism studies including hospitality, travel agency, tour operating management, airlines and would be of value to the students as also working professionals.

I am proud to present what I believe to be the most extensive and comprehensive publication of glossary of travel and tourism terms, acronyms and abbreviations available in one volume. It explains the operating language of the industry terms and would be useful to the diverse readership. Although the usefulness of the publication is diverse, the one important readership segment includes students in professional teaching and training programmes sponsored by tourism and related fields, those in college and university diploma and degree programmes and those seeking opportunities for continuing professional achievement and development.

The present volume has been prepared keeping in view the fact that there is no comprehensive similar publication available on the subject as of now. The publication has been developed taking into consideration the urge both of the student as also professionals in tourism industry to have clearer idea of different concepts of tourism terminology.

A.K. BHATIA

NEW DELHI

AUGUST - 2010

SECTION 1: A, B & C

Travel in general, airports, aviation, business travel, travel accounts, aircraft cabin, computer reservation system, airport formalities and miscellaneous.

A LA CARTE

A menu in which each food and drink item is separately priced and charged in a hotel/restaurant.

A MID SHIPS

In or toward the middle of the ship.

ABORT

Emergency procedure when an aircraft is stopped because there is danger in continuing. To cut short or end a pre-planned aircraft maneuver (i.e. aborted take off or aborted landing).

ACCESSIBILITY

The degree to which a market segment can be reached and served.

ACCIDENT, AVIATION

An occurrence on board an aircraft resulting in injury or death to one or more persons.

ACCOMMODATION, SUPPLEMENTARY

Various types of accommodation units other than the conventional hotel type. It includes accommodation for travellers in motels, youth hostels, camping sites etc. and is normally used by budget tourists.

ACCOMPANIED BAGGAGE

The baggage carried on the same aircraft as that on which the passenger is carried. As per the IATA regulations the weight of the accompanied baggage is fixed for different classes. Any excess baggage is to be paid for by the passenger.

ACCOUNTABLE TRAFFIC DOCUMENT

Paper value ticket, a miscellaneous charges order, a multiple purpose document whether issued or blank (excluding electronic formats).

ACCOUNTS, KEY

The most important accounts by sales volume / margin.

ACTIONABILITY

The degree to which effective programmes can be designed for attracting and serving a given market segment.

ADD-ON

Any additional component of a package tour that is not included in the package price.

ADJOINING

Two or more bed rooms next one to one but not connected by a common door.

ADMINISTERED VMS

A vertical marketing system that coordinates successive stages of production and distribution, not through common ownership or contractual ties, but through the size and power of one of the parties.

ADOPTION

The decision by a person to become a regular user of products.

ADULT

A person who has reached his/her 12th birthday as of the date of commencement of travel. A passenger is liable to pay full fare.

ADVANTAGE, COMPETITIVE

An advantage over competitors gained by offering consumers greater value either through lower prices or by providing more benefits that justify higher prices.

ADVERTISING, COMPARISON

Advertising that compares one brands directly or indirectly to one or more other brands.

ADVERTISING

Any paid form of non-personal presentation and promotion of ideas, goods, or services by an identified sponsor.

ADVERTISING SPECIALTIES

Useful articles imprinted with an advertiser's name given as gifts to consumers.

AERODROME

A defined area on land or water (including any buildings, installations, and equipment) intended to be used either wholly or in part for the arrival, departure and surface movement of aircraft. The term has evolved to refer to any surface used as an aircraft take off or landing facility.

AERODROME CONTROL

Directs the pilot in the vicinity of the airport and gives permission to land.

AFFINITY GROUP

A group bound together by common interest or affinity. Where charters are concerned, this common bond makes the concerned members eligible for charter flights. The group must travel together on the departure and return flights but can travel independently where ground arrangements are concerned.

AGE AND LIFE-CYCLE SEGMENTATION

Dividing a market into different age and life-cycle groups.

AGENT

A person authorized to act on behalf of another to transact business. For example, a travel agent is authorized by providers of services such as airlines, hotels, car rentals, tour operators, etc. to sell travel related services on their behalf.

AGENTS

An accredited passenger sales agent location selling tickets and travel services on behalf of its principals i.e. carriers both (domestic and international) and other travel service providers.

AGENTS, RETAIL

An agent who sells his individual travel services, e.g., accommodation, transportation, insurance etc., to the visitors.

AGRITOURISM

Farm based tourism helping to support the local agricultural economy. It is a style of vacation in which hospitality is offered on the farms.

AILERONS

A movable surface at the training edge of each airplane wing. They provide roll control and work opposite each other – when one goes up the other goes down and this provides the aircraft with the capability to turn either left or right. Controls located on the wings

AIR CARGO

Also known as air freight, consist of goods shipped by air, including letters, packages, cars, horses and construction equipment.

AIR NAVIGATION SERVICES (ANS)

The main function of airside airport operations that includes three types of services: air traffic control, flight information and alerting services.

AIR TRAFFIC CONTROL

The air Navigation Service that involves managing the airport movements of all airside vehicles and all aircraft, both on the ground and in the air.

AIR TRAFFIC CONTROLLER

A person working in air traffic control who is responsible for the safe, orderly, and expeditious flow of air traffic, in-flight or operating in the area of a runway.

AIR TRANSPORT INDUSTRY

The area of commerce that uses aircraft for the transport of people and cargo. This applies to flights of government-certified companies that offer services to the public and for general aviation, which applies to private aircraft used for business or recreation.

AIRBORN

When an aircraft is free from contact with the ground and is supporting itself in the air.

AIRFRAME

Consists of an airplane's wings; fuselage, or body; empennage, or tail assembly; and landing gear, or undercarriage.

AIRLINE

Any air transport enterprise offering or operating a scheduled international, domestic or regional service.

AIRLINES, COMMUTER

Regional airlines which offer transportation service between small, isolated communities unable to support larger aircraft.

AIRLINES, REGIONAL

Feeder airlines whose role is to bring passengers to the major hubs, where they will connect for longer distance flights on larger aircraft.

AIRPORT

An aerodrome that has been specifically licensed, for commercial aviation operations, by a responsible national government organization.

AIRPORT CODE

The three letter code given to each airport. Used in all airline schedules, manuals, and on baggage tags.

AIRPORT

Location where aircraft take-off and land, as well as load and unload passengers and cargo. Many of the larger airports have their own fire and law enforcement departments, customs and immigration and medical facilities along with retail and hotel establishments.

AIRPORT TAX (DEPARTURE TAX)

Charge levied by a city, state or country at the time of passenger's departure.

AIRPORTS, ALTERNATE

An airport other than the one originally scheduled as the destination airport. The alternate airport is used in the event that the aircraft cannot land at the original destination, usually due to adverse weather conditions.

AIRSIDE

Usually the side of the airport that has controlled access and is considered to be the secure side.

AIRSPACE, CONTROLLED

This is a part of airspace in which air traffic controllers maintain separation between airplanes. It is subdivided into three areas: Airway, Terminal Control Area and Control Zone.

AIRWAY

A controlled pathway or corridor of a flight, like a "highway on the sky".

AIRWAYS

These are published routes known as the highways of the sky. Upon reaching its assigned cruising altitude, an airplane flies along a predetermined flight path. Airplanes are not allowed to deviate from an airway unless authorized to do so by the local Air Traffic Control service.

AIRWORTHY

For the conditions for safe flight; an airworthiness certificate is issued by government authorities to indicate that an aircraft and its systems meet standards for safe operations.

AIRWAY BILL

Equivalent to the term "air consignment note" meaning the document entitled airway bill consignment note made out by or on behalf of the shipper which evidences contract between the shipper and carrier(s) for carriage of goods over routes of the carrier(s).

ALERTING SERVICES

The Air Navigation Service that notifies appropriate organizations when an airplane is missing or in trouble.

ALLIANCE

A formal agreement establishing an association between airlines to achieve a particular aim. This can allow companies to remain as separate entities, yet increase their efficiencies. Alliance allow for increased customer service with minimal increased cost to individual airlines.

ALLIANCES, STRATEGIC

Relationship between independent parties that agree to co-operate and still retain their separate identities. For instance strategic alliances between airlines for code share or frequent fliers programmes.

ALLOCENTRICS

Persons with a need for new experiences, such as backpackers and explorers.

ALLOWANCE, BAGGAGE

Refers to the amount of luggage each passenger is permitted to transport free of charge.

ALTERNATE AIRPORTS

An airport other than the one originally scheduled as the destination airport. The alternate airport is used in the event that the aircraft cannot land at the original destination, usually due to weather.

ALTERNATE TOURISM

A form of tourism that advocates smaller scale and limited tourism in terms of numbers of tourists involved and the dimension of tourism development. Also called responsible tourism.

ALTERNATIVE EVALUATION

The stages of the buyer decision process in which a consumer uses information to evaluate alternative brands in the choice set.

AMENITIES

Small complimentary items kept in the guest rooms of a hotel. Goods and services offered that improve the comfort and overall experience of passengers. The amenities include food and beverage facilities, drinking water, good communication network, local transport, proper garbage disposal systems, medical facilities etc. available at the destination.

AMERICAN SOCIETY OF TRAVEL AGENTS (ASTA)

American Society of Travel Agents (ASTA) is a business improvement organization which represents and defends the business and regulatory public policy interests of travel intermediaries and operators.

Its members include travel agents and intermediaries as well as supplier companies who offer travel products and services such as tours, cruises, hotels, destinations, tourist bureaus, ground transport, car rentals, local guides and hosts, etc. ASTA calls itself the leading advocate for travel agents, the travel industry and the travelling public. ASTA claims over 20,000 total members in 140 countries and is headquartered in Alexandria, Virginia, USA. ASTA is governed by a 15 member US-based Board of Directors drawn from its voting eligible membership.

AMOUNT, ADD-ON

An amount used only to construct an unspecified through fare.

ANALYSIS, BREAKEVEN

Financial calculation that shows the number of units that need to be sold to cover costs.

ANALYSIS, COMPETITIVE

An analysis of the primary strengths and weaknesses, objectives, strategies, and other information relative to competitors.

ANALYSIS, SEGMENTATION

The process of examining various sub markets and selecting those most appropriate for a company.

ANTIQUITIES

Art objects which are more than one hundred year old and which cannot be traded.

APARTMENTS

A room or a set of rooms fitted especially with house keeping facilities and usually leased as a dwelling. A building containing several individual apartments.

APEX FARES

Advance purchase excursion fare which is purchased in advance of undertaking the journey. The fare is non-refundable and certain conditions apply.

APEX

Advance purchase excursion fare. This airfare has to be purchased from fourteen days to two months in advance. It is generally available on a return basis only with minimum and maximum stay requirements. No stopovers are allowed and there are cancellation charges.

APPROACH CONTROL UNIT (ACU)

Keep air traffic moving smoothly and safely in the airspace surrounding a major aerodrome.

APPROVERS

People who authorize the proposed actions, deciders or buyers.

AREA CONTROL CENTRE (ACC)

Provides air traffic services to controlled flights within a designated controlled area.

AREA, BAGGAGE CLAIM

An area of an airport where arriving passengers can collect their baggage brought with them in the flight.

ARRANGEMENTS, LAND

All services provided for the traveller by his tour operator after the traveller reaches his first foreign destination. Does not apply to overseas travel. Also referred to as ground arrangements.

ARRIVALS AREA

Passengers enter this area as they leave the aircraft where they will encounter immigration, customs and baggage claim.

ASPIRATIONAL GROUP

A group to which a person wishes to belong.Normally this group consists of members having common interests.

ATMOSPHERE

Designed environments that create or reinforce a buyer's leanings toward consumption of a product.

ATTITUDE

A person's enduring favourable or unfavourable cognitive evaluations, emotional feelings, and action tendencies toward some object or idea.

ATTRACTIONS AND AMENITIES

Services needed by the tourists at the destination or resort. These are usually built and might be stately home, an activity centre, a theme park or even a catering facility such as food outlet or five star restaurant.

ATTRACTIONS

Natural or built features of a destination which singly or collectively create the appeal of a destination.

ATTRACTIONS, BUILT

This category of tourist attraction is much larger in scope and variety. At one extreme are large cities with a wealth of historical buildings and museums. At the other extreme is a small monument or shrine dedicated to a well-known person.

ATTRACTIONS, NATURAL

These are well-defined natural features of a region. Visitors are generally drawn towards beautiful scenery, high mountains, forests, rivers, lakes coastlines and similar outstanding features.

AUTHORITY, IMMIGRATION

Agency that monitors persons entering or leaving the country by validating appropriate documentation to allow entry to the country or to forbid entry to the country. The immigration authority has the right to forbid entry into the country because of missing documentation or because the person is a possible threat. In some countries Immigration is a separate agency from Customs.

AUTOMATED TICKET/ BOARDING PASS (ATB)

Form of automated ticket and boarding pass. It is a single copy non-carbonized ticket (normally on card stock) with each coupon imprinted separately. Each coupon used for air transport is comprised of a flight coupon and a detachable passenger coupon and boarding pass for a specific flight. One coupon is issued as the passenger receipt which together with all passenger coupons and boarding passes builds up the passenger copy of the passenger ticket and baggage check.

AVAILABILITY, SEAT

Term used to indicate the number of unutilized seats remaining for purchase.

AVAILABLE SEAT KILOMETRE (ASK) COST

Operating cost to fly one aircraft seat one kilometre.

AVAILABLE SEAT KILOMETRE (ASK)

A measure of capacity available. The available seat kilometre is calculated by multiplying the number of seats available on a flight leg by the number of kilometres flown during that flight leg.

AVIATION ACCIDENT

An occurrence on board an aircraft resulting in injury or death to one or more persons.

AVIATION INCIDENT

An occurrence other than an accident, associated with the operation of an aircraft, which affects or could affect the safety of operations.

AVIATION INDUSTRY

The range of activities involved in building and flying aircraft. These include aircraft manufacturing, airport operations, and aviation support industries.

AVIATION SAFETY

Refers to the efforts that are taken to ensure airplanes are free from factors that may lead to injury or loss.

AVIATION SAFETY REPORTING SYSTEM (ASRS)

A means of promoting air safety within the industry. This is a voluntary system that allows pilots and other airplane crew members to anonymously report near misses and close calls in the interest of improving air safety.

AVIATION SECURITY

A combination of measures and human and material resources intended to safeguard civil aviation against acts of unlawful interference.

AVIATION

The science and practice of flight and airplanes. Aviation is grouped into three broad classes: Commercial, General and Military.

AVIATION, BUSINESS

The transportation of passengers, as well as cargo, for business purposes. Sometimes referred to as corporate aviation.

AVIATION, CIVIL

The broad segment of aviation that includes commercial and private aviation, as well as general aviation, but excludes military aviation.

AVIONICS

The science and technology of electronics and the development of electronic devices as applied to aeronautics and astronautics.

BACK OF THE HOUSE

The area of the hotel not accessible to the public but can be used only by authorized employees.

BACK OFFICE STAFF

These are employees whose primary employment objective is to support the front line personnel who deliver a service.

BACKSTAGE

Metaphor for the area of the service setting away from the audience's inspection, where much of the planning and execution of the service experience occurs.

BACKWARD INTEGRATION

A growth strategy by which companies acquire businesses that supply them with products or services, such as restaurant chain purchasing a bakery.

BAGGAGE ACCOMPANIED

Baggage travelling on the same aircraft as the passenger.

BAGGAGE ALLOWANCE

Refers to the amount of luggage each passenger is permitted to transport free of charge.

BAGGAGE CHECK

Means those portions of the tickets, which relate to the carriage of the passenger's checked baggage.

BAGGAGE CLAIM AREA

An area of an airport where arriving passengers can collect their baggage brought with them in the flight.

BAGGAGE TAG

A document indicating the passengers name and address that is attached to the luggage as means of identification at the time of retrieving the baggage on arrival at the destination.

BAGGAGE, EXCESS

A passenger's baggage presented at check in counter of an airline that is in excess (either in terms of weight or dimensions) of free allowance on which charges are to be paid.

BAGGAGE, UNACCOMPANIED

The baggage not carried on the same aircraft as that on which the passenger is carried.

BAGGAGE

Personal items carried by a traveller, such as clothes, camera, equipment and other articles related to the journey.

BALANCE SHEET

A statement of assets and liabilities.

BANK, CLEARING

The bank or other organization appointed under BSP to perform all or some of the following functions: to receive sales transmittals from Agents, and to extract and process date therefrom, to render billings to Agents, to receive remittances from Agents and to perform such other functions. It may also mean the processing centre where the context so permits.

BANKERS BUYING RATE

(BBR): the rate at which, for the purpose of the transfer of funds through banking channels (i.e. other than transactions in bank notes, travellers cheques and similar banking instruments), a bank will PURCHASE a given amount of foreign currency in exchange for one unit (or units) of the national currency of the country in which the exchange transaction takes place.

BANKERS SELLING RATE

(BSR) the rate at which, for the purpose of the transfer of funds through banking channels (i.e. other than transactions in bank notes, travellers cheques and similar banking instruments), a bank will SELL a given amount of foreign currency in exchange for one unit (or units) of the national currency of the country in which the exchange transaction takes place.

BAR-CODED BOARDING PASSES (BCBP)

Allows customers to print their own boarding pass at home, or at the office, and thus avoid queues for check-in. All they will have to do at check-in is go to a self-service kiosk.

BEACH RESORT

A self-contained site which provides all or most of the products and services required by guest (a tourist). These tend to combine attractions with support services such as accommodation and catering.

BED AND BREAKFAST

A hotel meal plan where breakfast is included in the cost of rent of a room.

BEHAVIOUR SEGMENTATION

Dividing a market into groups based on consumers' knowledge, attitude, use, or response to a product.

BEHAVIOUR, POST - PURCHASE

The stage of the buyer decision process in which consumers take further action after the purchase based on their satisfaction or dissatisfaction.

BELIEF

A descriptive thought that a person holds about something.

BELL STAND

A portion of the lobby set aside for receiving luggage and distributing it to all the guests in their rooms.

BENEFIT SEGMENTATION

Dividing the market into groups according to the different benefits that consumers seek from the product.

BENEFIT

What a product or service will do for someone.

BERMUDA PLAN (B P)

Hotel accommodation with a full American style breakfast included in the room rate.

BERTH

1. Dock or pier. 2. The bed or beds within the passenger cabins.

BERTH

The ship's placement at a dock; a margin of safety, as in, "allow a wide berth"; a bed.

BILGE

The lowest part of the ship's hull; location of most crew housing.

BILL, AIRWAY

Equivalent to the term "air consignment note" meaning the document entitled airway bill consignment note made out by or on behalf of the shipper which evidences contract between the shipper and carrier(s) for carriage of goods over routes of the carrier(s).

BILLING AND SETTLEMENT PLAN (BSP)

A reporting system for collecting ticket payments from travel agents and distributing the funds to the appropriate airlines on whose behalf tickets have been sold.

BIO-DIVERSITY

A variety of wildlife in a particular area / region.

BIOMETRIC VISA

It requires statistical analyses of biological observations and phenomenon. The process takes finger scans and a digital photograph as part of the visa application process. The process is to proof and protects that customers from identity brand. The unauthorized persons will not be able to access the biometric data and the data will not be used inappropriately.

BIRD STRIKE

An aviation description for a collision between a bird and an aircraft. It is a common threat to aircraft safety and has caused a number of fatal accidents.

BLACK BOX

The Black Box on an airplane is not black in colour but orange for better visibility. There are two black boxes. The important one is the Flight Data Recorder which records time, altitude, air speed, pitch and other data .The second box is the Cockpit Voice Recorder, which records pilot's conversation and other sounds in the cockpit .Black boxes are placed near tail of the plane to minimize impact damage.

BLITZ, SALES

A concentrated burst of sales activity within a specific area by a group of sales people, such as many persons in one territory.

BOOKING FORM

A form completed by a travel agent when a booking is created. The form records details of the customer's name, contact address and telephone number, itinerary, payment details, and booking conditions.

BOOKINGS, GROUP

A set of rooms set-aside for groups of ten or more people and negotiated at special price. This negotiated price is lower than the normal price.

BOUNDARY SPANNERS

The front-stage employees who link an organization with its customers.

BOUTIQUE HOTEL

A term popularised in North America and the United Kingdom to describe intimate, usually luxurious hotel environments. Boutique hotels differentiate themselves from larger chain/branded hotels and motels by providing personalized accommodation and services/ facilities. Sometimes known as "design hotels" or "lifestyle hotels", boutique hotels began appearing in the 1980s in major cities like London, New York, and San Francisco. Typically boutique hotels are furnished in a themed, stylish and/or aspirational manner. They usually are considerably smaller than mainstream hotels, often ranging from 3 to 50 guest rooms.

Boutique hotels are always individual and are therefore extremely unlikely to be found amongst the homogeneity of large chain hotel groups. Guest rooms and suites may be fitted with telephony and Wi-Fi Internet, air-conditioning, and often cable/pay TV, but equally may have none of these, focusing on quiet and comfort rather than gadgetry. Guest services are often attended to by 24-hour hotel staff. Many boutique hotels have on-site dining facilities, and the majority offer bars and lounges that may also be open to the general public.

BOW

Front or forward portion of the ship.

BRAND

A name, term, sign, symbol, or design or a combination of these intended to identify the goods or services of one seller or group of sellers and to differentiate them from those of competitors.

BRAND IMAGE

The set of beliefs consumers hold about a particular branded product.

BREAK EVEN PRICING (TARGET PROFIT PRICING)

Setting price to break even on the costs of making and marketing a product or to make the desired profit.

BREAK – EVEN LOAD FACTOR

The break even load factor of an airline is a level where revenue earned per passenger per kilometer equals the cost incurred in doing so. A load factor higher than the break – even point contributes to airline's profitability.

BREAK – EVEN POINT

The point at which revenues are equal to expenses.

BREAK – EVEN ANALYSIS

Financial calculation that shows the number of units that need to be sold to cover costs.

BREAKFAST, CONTINENTAL

This generally consists of a beverage (coffee, tea, cocoa or milk) plus rolls, butter or jam or marmalade, toast and pastry and perhaps fresh seasonal fruits as part of room tariff.

BREAKFAST, ENGLISH

This type of breakfast is generally served in Great Britain. It usually includes hot or cold cereal, bacon or ham and eggs, toast, butter, jam or marmalade and beverage (though not juice).

BRIDGE

Where the steering and navigation equipment are located.

BROCHURE

A pamphlet bound in the form of a booklet containing detailed information about a product / service.

BROKERS

Brokers are intermediaries between carriers and operators. They obtain seats or, in some cases, complete aircraft, on behalf of smaller tour operators or clients and can save these organizations in considerable time and expense because of the contacts they have.

BUILT ATTRACTIONS

This category of tourist attraction is much larger in scope and variety. At one extreme are large cities with a wealth of historical buildings and museums. At the other extreme is a small monument or shrine dedicated to a well-known person.

BULKHEAD

A vertical wall or partition of the passenger's cabin in a ship or aircraft.

BULLETIN

Brief, periodically issued mailing or promotion piece, often devoted to trade news.

BUNGEE JUMPING

An adventure sport which requires no equipment other than bungee chord made of nylon fibre of enough elasticity to be able to absorb the shock at the end of the jump. The only infrastructure required is a bridge or any structure which offers few hundred feet of free fall.

BUREAU, CONVENTION

A non - profit marketing organization that promotes a city or region to the convention and meetings markets.

BUSINESS ANALYSIS

A review of the sales, costs, and profit projections for a new product to find out whether they satisfy the company's objectives.

BUSINESS AVIATION

The transportation of passengers, as well as cargo, for business purposes. Sometimes referred to as corporate aviation.

BUSINESS AVIATION

The sector of aviation which concerns the operation or use of aircraft by companies for the carriage of passengers or goods as an aid to the conduct of their business, flown for purposes generally considered not for public hire and piloted by individuals having at the minimum, a valid commercial pilot license with an instrument rating.

BUSINESS CLASS

Also referred to as "C" or "J class. Several airlines have their own terminology. The fare for this class is higher than that of Economy Class commiserating with the comfort and services offered.

BUSINESS TOURISM

Business tourism is concerned with people travelling for purposes, which are related to their work. As such it represents the oldest forms of tourism, man having travelled for this purpose of trade, since very early times in the history.

BUSINESS TRAVEL

Business Travel is the act of travelling for purposes which are related to their work, like meetings, conferences and conventions on behalf of the corporate entity or business at its expense. Business travel is that category of tourism in which travellers visit distant destination within their own country or outside the country to conduct their business activities. This could involve attending meetings, participating in seminars; conferences and conventions as also trade fairs and exhibitions.

BUSINESS VISITOR

A business visitor includes a person who visits a country to transact business, including attending meetings and briefing, fact finding negotiating or making contacts with business to buy or sell goods or services. The list of typical business visitors also includes those visiting a country to purchase trade goods and those visiting for training in techniques and work practices, provided that the training is confined to observation, familiarization and classroom instructions.

BUYER READINESS STAGES

The stages consumers normally pass through on their way to purchase, including awareness, knowledge, liking, preferences, conviction, and purchase.

BUYER

The person who makes an actual purchase; (one who has formal authority for selecting suppliers and arranging the terms of purchase).

BUYING CENTRE

All those individuals and groups who participate in the purchasing and decision making process, who share common goals and the risks arising from the decisions.

BUYING INFLUENCE

Either an individual or a group within a category that has a decision-making role in a large-account sale.

CABIN ATTENDANT

Also known as Cabin Crew /Flight Attendant are the Staff who care for passengers on board the aircraft and maintain safety and service during flight.

CABIN

The interior of the aircraft where passengers are seated.

CABOTAGE FARE

Special reduced fares known as "Cabotage Fares" are available but only to the nationals of the territories qualifying as Cabotage traffic.

CABOTAGE

Cabotage may be defined as the carriage of the passengers and goods between two points of a state's territory. The state's "territories" may be defined as being within the mother country, between the mother country and its colonies and its protectorates. The state concerned will normally restrict such carriage of the state(s) concerned but some expectations to this rule do exist.

CAMPAIGN

A connected, integrated and organised series of advertising and promotional efforts.

CAMPING SITE

A place providing simple and inexpensive shelter to travellers. The site provides waybill amenities for tourists travelling by long distance coach tours and self-driven cars.

CANCELLATION CHARGE

Means the service charge made by reason of failure of a passenger to use reserved accommodation without having cancelled such accommodation prior to the latest appropriate time for cancellation specified by the carrier.

CANCELLATION FEE

Penalty levied by airlines when a passenger fails to use a reservation.The quantum of cancellation fee varies depending upon time of cancellation.

CAPACITY MANAGEMENT

Managing the number of seats in aircrafts owned or operated by an airline.

CAPACITY, CARRYING

The maximum number of people who can use a site without an unacceptable alteration to the physical environment and without an unacceptable decline in the quality of experience gained by visitors.

"The concept of maintaining a level of development and use that will not result in serious environment deterioration, socio-cultural or economic problems, or be perceived by tourists depreciating their enjoyment and appreciation of the area." UNWTO

That level of tourist presence which creates impacts on the host community, environment and economy that is acceptable to both tourists and hosts, and sustainable over future time periods.

CAPSULE HOTEL

In the Capsule Hotel, the guest space is reduced in size to a modular plastic or fiberglass block roughly 2 m by 1 m by 1.25 m, providing room to sleep. Facilities range in entertainment offerings (most include a television, an electronic console, and wireless internet connection). These capsules are stacked side by side and two units top to bottom, with steps providing access to the second level rooms. Luggage is stored in a locker, usually somewhere outside of the hotel. Privacy is ensured by a curtain or a fiberglass door at the open end of the capsule. Washrooms are common and most hotels include restaurants (or at least vending machines), pools, and other entertainment facilities.

This style of hotel accommodation was developed in Japan and has not gained popularity outside of the country, although Western variants with larger accommodations and often private baths are being developed. Guests are asked not to smoke or eat in the capsules.

These capsule hotels vary widely in size, some having only fifty or so capsules and others over 700. Many are used primarily by men. There are also capsule hotels with separate male and female sleeping quarters. Clothes and shoes are sometimes exchanged for a yukata and slippers on entry. A towel may also be provided. The benefit of these hotels is convenience and price.

The first capsule hotel was the Capsule Inn Osaka, designed by Kisho Kurokawa and located in the Umeda district of Osaka. It opened on February 1, 1971.

CARAVAN

A vehicle or a large covered van with facilities for the passengers usually owners to live inside for a short period when travelling primarily for the purpose of tourism.It may also be used for recreational purposes and also called as recreational vehicle.

CARGO AIRLINES

Also known as the Airfreighter Carriers, these are airlines dedicated to the transport of cargo. Some cargo airlines are divisions or subsidiaries of larger passenger airlines.

CARGO, AIR

Also known as air freight, consist of goods shipped by air, including letters, packages, cars, horses and construction equipment.

CARGO

Equivalent to the word 'goods' meaning anything carried or to be carried in an aircraft other than mail or baggage moving under an airway bill is also cargo.

CARRIAGE DOMESTIC

Carriage in which according to the contract of carriage, the place of departure, the place of destination or stopover and the entire transportation are within one nation or its territories.

CARRIAGE INTERNATIONAL

Carriage in which according to the contract of carriage, the place of departure, and any place of landing are situated in more than one nation. As used in this definition, the term national includes all territory subject to the sovereignty, mandate, authority or trust – ship thereof.

CARRIAGE

Equivalent to term 'Transportation' means carriage of passengers and / or baggage by air gratuitously or for hire.

CARRIER, PARTICIPATING

Means a carrier over whose routes one or more sections of carriage under the ticket is undertaken or performed.

CARRIER

A passenger or cargo transportation company.

CARRYING CAPACITY

The maximum number of people that a resort, site or other area can sustain, before there is a reduction in the quality of the visitor experience or adverse effects on either physical environment or host community.

CAST MEMBERS

A term used for employees. It means that employees are part of a team that is performing for the guests.

CASUAL RESEARCH

Marketing research to rest hypotheses about and-effect-relationships.

CASUAL- COMPARATIVE RESEARCH

Also known as ex-post-facto research. This is a research that attempts to determine the cause, or reason, for existing differences in the behaviour or status of groups of individuals. It usually involves starting with and effect and seeking possible causes.

CATEGORIES, RATE

Rate categories indicate the amount of money hotels charge for a room and the various discounts available within the initially quoted price.

CATEGORY

A price gradient of similar cabins from the most expensive to the least expensive or vice-versa.

CATERING

Food, beverages and gallery supplies brought to the aircraft for a flight. Catering or Commissary also refers to the department responsible for handling all food, beverages and supplies.

CENTRE, BUYING

All those individuals and groups who participate in the purchasing and decision making process, who share common goals and the risks arising from the decisions.

CENTRAL RESERVATION OFFICE (CRO)

Central Reservation Office is a call centre for hotel companies.

CENTRE, TOURIST

A village or town with a definite concentration of tourist resources, material base and infrastructure of tourism development.

CHAIN

A group of hotels managed and / or owned by one organization.

CHAIR, DECK

Open deck chaise longue which is generally provided on a complementary basis.

CHANNEL CONFLICT

Disagreement among marketing channel members on goals and roles on who should do what and for what rewards.

CHANNEL LEVEL

A layer of middlemen that perform some work in bringing the product and its ownership closer to the final buyer.

CHANNEL, DISTRIBUTION

A set of independent organizations involved in the process of making a product or service available for use or consumption by a consumer or business user.

CHARGE, CANCELLATION

The service charge made by reason of failure of a passenger to use reserved accommodation without having cancelled such accommodation prior to the latest appropriate time for cancellation specified by the carrier.

CHARGES, RELATED

Such as cancellation penalties, non-refundable amounts, rebooking and rerouting charges, stopover charges, weekend surcharges etc. & excess baggage charges.

CHARTER (FLIGHTS)

The contract for the complete and exclusive use of an aircraft. The term often refers to flights operated by tour companies to resort or popular holiday destinations during high season.

CHARTER AIRLINES

Also sometime referred to as air taxi, these airlines operate aircraft on a charter basis, that is flights that take place outside normal schedule, by a hiring arrangement with a particular customer.

CHARTER FLIGHTS

Non-scheduled flights typically for travellers who want to hire a plane to fly to a specific place at a specific time. A charter airline operates these flights that take place outside normal schedules through hiring arrangements with a particular customer.

CHARTER, TOURIST

A flight booked exclusively for the use of a specific group of tourists who generally belong to the same organization or who are being 'treated' to the flight by a single host.

CHECK IN (HOTEL)

System of registration upon arrival in a hotel. The check-in time in classified hotel across the world is 1200 noon.

CHECK IN

Various formalities in connection with flight undertaken by a passenger at an airport before departure. These formalities include the checking of passenger documents, allocation of seats and issue of boarding cards and baggage tags.

CHECK OUT

System of payment upon departure from the hotel. The check out time in classified hotels across the world is 1200 noon.

CHECK, BAGGAGE

Those portions of the tickets, which relate to the carriage of the passenger's checked baggage.

CHECK-CALL-CARE

The three steps to remember when providing first aid. These steps give the responder an easy and safe approach to providing first aid for a victim.

CHECK-IN

A process at thc airport, which includes checking documents, issuing a boarding pass and accepting baggage and permitting the passenger to go to the departure lounge and board the plane when announced by an airline. In the hospitality industry check-in refers to greeting and registering a guest, verifying the method of payment and handing over room keys.

CHECKED –IN BAGGAGE

Baggage handed over by the traveller and accepted by an international carrier, in the same carrier in which he /she is travelling and for which the baggage receipt has been issued as a proof.

CHICAGO CONVENTION

The treaty that governs the conduct of international civil aviation and is constantly being amended.

CHILD

A person who has reached his/her second birthday but not his/her 12th birthday as of the date of commencement of travel.

CIRCLE TRIP FOR NORMAL FARES

Travel from and to the same point by a continuous, circuitous air route which may have 2 or more fare components which do not meet the round trip definition.

CIRCLE TRIPS FOR SPECIAL FARES

Travel from and to the same point by a continuous, circuitous air route, comprising two international fare components which do not meet the conditions of the round trip definitions.

CIVIL AVIATION

The broad segment of aviation that includes commercial and private aviation, as well as general aviation, but excludes military aviation.

CLASS, BUSINESS

Referred to as "C" or "J". Several airlines have their own terminology. The fare for this class is higher than that of Economy Class commensurating with the comfort and services offered.

CLASS, ECONOMY

Symbolized by "Y". This is difficult to classify except when used for excursion fares. Sometimes referred to a full fare, particularly when business class facilities are not available.

CLEARING BANK

The bank or other organization appointed under BSP to perform all or some of the following functions: to receive sales transmittals from Agents, and to extract and process date therefrom, to render billings to Agents, to receive remittances from Agents and to perform such other functions. It may also mean the processing centre where the context so permits.

CLIENT

A person to whom you provide a product and/or service.

CLIFF DIVING

The act of diving from a high cliff into a river, lake or ocean below the cliff. It has been practiced as an unorganized activity both for recreation and other purposes. It is an organized sport, with large-scale competitions held in several places of the world. Cliff diving is classified as an extreme sport because of the inherent dangers.

CLIMATE

A weather pattern that characteristically prevails in a region over a long period of time.

CLIMBING, ROCK

Climbing straight flat rock. The activity can be performed in areas which have rock formation.

CLOSED-END QUESTIONS

Questions that include all the possible answers and allow subjects to make choices among them.

CLOSING

Any process involving getting the prospect to commit to paying for the product or service.

CNS/ATM SYSTEMS

Acronyms for communications, Navigation, Surveillance / Air Traffic Management Systems, a navigation network of satellite and ground based systems.

CO - RELATIONAL RESEARCH

Attempts to determine whether, and to what degree, a relationship exists between two or more quantifiable variables. The purpose is to establish a relationship (or lack of it) or to use relationships in making predictions.

CO-OPERATIVE PRINT ADVERTISING

A form of shared promotion between several travel professionals or organizations wherein the co-operating organization or individuals share the expense of a single print advertisement.

COACH TOUR

A guided bus tour for a group of holiday makers that follows a scheduled itinerary. Visitors purchase all arrangements from the in–bound tour operator prior to arrival at the destination.

COCKPIT (FLIGHT DECK)

The area of the aircraft where all the controls and navigational equipment to fly the aircraft are located. It is where the pilot and co-pilot sit.

COCKPIT VOICE RECORDERS (CVRs)

Devices which record conversations and sounds throughout an aircraft's cockpit on digital tape or on a digital microchip.

CODE, AIRPORT

The three letter code given to each airport. Used in all airline schedules, manuals, and on baggage tags.

CODE SHARING

Each airline is identified by a code assigned to it. Code sharing is marketing alliance between two carriers. Under such an arrangement, an airline can sell its seats in their own name on sectors it does not have operations by booking tickets on the flights operated by the airline with which it has a code sharing pact.

For example, if a person intending to travel to Berlin in Germany has gone to Air India's website than he or she would find a flight even if the national carrier does not operate to the German capital. The passenger would locate the Lufthansa flight on Air India's website as the two have a code – share agreement. Without the arrangement, airlines would loose traffic to bigger rivals. Such an arrangement is extremely beneficial for smaller airlines.

CODE SHARE

The term is popularly used in airline industry. A single flight on which space is shared and sold by two airlines. A ticket may be issued under the code of either airline and the flight may have two flight numbers.

CODE-SHARING

This enables the passengers to fly a segment of their trip on an airplane other than the airplane that sold the ticket for the flight.

COGNITIVE DISSONANCE

Buyer discomfort caused by post purchase conflict.

COLLATERAL

Promotional materials such as brochures, DVD's and posters, distributed to travel trade partners for the purpose of educating sellers about and/or assisting in the sale of supplier's products.

COMBINATION

Whenever two or more one-way or round trip or half round trip fares are used and shown separately in a fare calculation.

COMMERCIAL FLIGHT

A regularly scheduled flight carrying passengers and/or cargo.

COMMERCIAL HOTEL

Establishment catering to individuals on business and for tourists staying for a short time. The hotel provides a comfortable sleeping accommodation and meal services, ranging from modest rooms and a coffee shop to elegant suites and a first class specialty restaurant. This also includes additional facilities such as conference room, a banquet hall, business centre, etc. In big cities these hotels are generally located near the business districts or in the centre of the city.

COMMERCIAL TRANSPORT PLANES

The large planes owned or leased by an airline company designed specifically to carry passengers and cargo (or just cargo). The smallest can carry from 20 to 100 passengers and the largest can carry several hundred. Most of these planes are jet planes with two or three or four engines.

COMMERCIALIZATION

Introducing a new product into the market.

COMMISSION

Amount of money earned by agents from sale of flight and other services like insurance, hotel rooms etc. Commission is usually a percentage of the sale price.

COMMON USE SELF SERVICE (CUSS)

Standard that allows airlines to share self-service kiosks and passengers to enjoy the same convenience they have with bank ATM (Automatic Teller Machine) dispensers.

COMMUNICATION, CORPORATE

The activity which covers internal and external communications and promotes understanding of an organization.

COMMUTER AIRLINES

Regional airlines which offer transportation service between small, isolated communities unable to support larger aircraft.

COMPACT DISC (CD)

An optical disc used to store digital data, originally developed for storing digital audio.

COMPARISON ADVERTISING

Advertising that compares one brands directly or indirectly to one or more other brands.

COMPETITIVE ADVANTAGE

An advantage over competitors gained by offering consumers greater value either through lower prices or by providing more benefits that justify higher prices.

COMPETITIVE ANALYSIS

An analysis of the primary strengths and weaknesses, objectives, strategies, and other information relative to competitors.

COMPETITIVE PARITY METHOD

Setting the promotion budget to match competitors' outlays.

COMPLEMENTARY SERVICES

Services that accompany a core product and support its acquisition usage and / or disposition.

COMPONENT, FARE

A portion of an itinerary between two consecutive fare construction points.

COMPUTER RESERVATION SYSTEM (CRS)

A method of recording and processing reservations and issuing tickets using a computer rather than a manual paper based method. A computerized system is used to access information about schedules, availability, fares and other travel formalities. A CRS is a means of communication between agents and airlines, through which reservations can be made and tickets and itineraries issued.

CONCENTRATED MARKETING

A market-coverage strategy in which a firm goes after a large share of one or few submarkets.

CONCENTRIC DIVERSIFICATION STRATEGY

A growth strategy whereby a company seeks new products that have technological and marketing synergies with existing products lines.

CONCEPT, MARKETING

The marketing management philosophy which holds that achieving organizational goals depends on determining the needs and wants of target markets and delivering desired satisfactions more effectively and efficiently than competitors.

CONCIERGE

A hotel employee who handles restaurant and tour reservations, travel arrangements and other details for hotel guests.

CONCIERGE

A staff member who provides assistance for guests such as help in obtaining theatre and other entertainment tickets, renting a car, arranging sight seeing. Also known as hall porter.

CONDITIONS

Refers to a booking and the rules of contract between, for example: an agent and his client. Relates to cancellation / administration charges, date change conditions, passport, visa and health requirements. In addition, any other general terms and conditions established by travel agencies or carriers.

CONDITIONS OF CARRIAGE

The terms and conditions established by a carrier in respect to its carriage.

CONDITIONS OF CONTRACT

The term and conditions shown on the passenger ticket and baggage check.

CONDUCTOR, TOUR

Person employed to escort members of a tourist group for the entire journey. Also called Leader, Escort, and Courier.

CONFIDENTIAL TARIFF

Discounted prices quoted to wholesalers, tour operators and travel agents in confidence and not published for public use.

CONFIGURATION

The seating arrangements of the aircraft.

CONFIRMATION

Written acknowledgement of reservation often indicated by a number or code.

CONFIRMED RESERVATION

Oral or written statement by a supplier that the request for a reservation has been received and will be honored.

CONNECTING

Two or more sleeping rooms with a common door between them.

CONSOLIDATORS

Based on some offshore markets, Consolidators buy airfares in bulk from airlines and sell these to retail agents for on-sale to consumers.

CONSORTIUM RATE

Negotiated rates based on volume.

CONSTRUCTED FARE

Unspecified through fares created by the use of add-on amounts, or two or more fares shown as a single amount in a fare calculation.

CONSUMER FRANCHISE BUILDING PROMOTIONS

Sales promotions that promotes a product's positioning and include a selling message along with the deal.

CONSUMER PROMOTION

Sales promotions designed to stimulate consumer purchasing, including samples, coupons, rebates, prices-off, premiums, patronage rewards, displays, and sweepstakes.

CONSUMERISM

An organised movement of citizens and government to strengthen the right and power of buyers in relation to sellers.

CONTESTS, SWEEPSTAKES, AND GAMES

Promotional events that give consumers the chance to win something such as cash, trips, or goods by luck or through extra effort.

CONTINENTAL BREAKFAST

This generally consists of a beverage (coffee, tea, cocoa or milk) plus rolls, butter or jam or marmalade.

OR

It includes tea, coffee and juices, toast, butter, jam and pastry and perhaps fresh seasonal fruit as part of room tariff.

CONTROL ZONE

A cylindrical block of airspace, centred on the aerodrome, with an 8 Km radius, extending from the ground to about 3000 m above seas level. Within this airspace, a control tower provides control, information and alert services to all aircraft in flight or operating on the maneuvering area, and control service to vehicles on the ground.

CONTROL, AERODROME

Directs the pilot in the vicinity of the airport and gives permission to land.

CONTROL, AIR TRAFFIC (ATC)

The official authority in charge of the safe, orderly, and expeditious flow of air traffic in-flight or operating in the area of a runway.

CONTROL, AIR TRAFFIC

The air navigation service that involves managing the airport movements of all airside vehicles and all aircraft, both on the ground and in the air.

CONTROLLABLE MARKETING VARIABLES

Factors that the service organization can manage in its effort to deliver service excellence.

CONTROLLED AIRSPACE

This is a part of airspace in which air traffic controllers maintain separation between airplanes. It is subdivided into three areas: Airway, Terminal Control Area and Control Zone.

CONTROLLED FLIGHT INTO TERRAIN (CFIT)

This is a class of accident in which an undamaged aircraft is seemingly flown, under control, into terrain, such as a mountain, the ocean, or the ground.

CONTROLLER, AIR TRAFFIC

A person working in air traffic control and is responsible for the safe, orderly, and expeditious flow of air traffic, in-flight or operating in the area of a runway.

CONVENTION

A specialty market requiring extensive meeting facilities. It is usually the annual meeting of an association and includes general sessions, committee meetings, and special-interest sessions.

CONVENTION BUREAU

A nonprofit marketing organization that promotes a city or region to the convention and meetings markets.

CONVENTION CENTRE

A place or a venue for organising large conventions. Convention Centre are located centrally offering state of art facilities for the proper and efficient meetings and are accessible to airports having ample parking facility.

CONVENTION, CHICAGO

The treaty that governs the conduct of international civil aviation and is constantly being amended.

CONVENTION

An assembly of people meeting formally to discuss common issues concerning their business and thereafter formulate policies. Conventions are normally annual events and are attended by a large number of people.

CORAL REEFS

Coral reefs are aragonite structures produced by living animal colonies, found in marine waters containing few nutrients. Reefs grow best in shallow, clear, sunny and agitated waters. The accumulation of skeletal material, broken and piled up by wave action and bioeroders, produces formation that supports the living corals and a great variety of other animal and plant life.

Often called "rainforests of the sea", coral reefs form some of the richest and most diverse ecosystems on earth. They occupy less than one percent of the world ocean surface, about half the area of France, yet they provide a home for 25% of all marine species, including fishes, molluscs, echinoderms and sponges.

CORE PRODUCT

The central feature or benefit sought by the customer and offered by the service provider as a solution to customers' needs or wants.

CORPORATE IMAGE ADVERTISING

A corporate image advertising is designed to primarily promote the enterprise and secondarily promote the products and services of the enterprise.

CORPORATE COMMUNICATION

The activity which covers internal and external communications and promotes understanding of an organization.

CORPORATE MEETING

A meeting held by a corporation for its employees.

CORPORATE MISSION STATEMENT

A guide to provide all the publics of a company with a shared sense of purpose, direction, and opportunity that allows all to work independently, yet collectively, toward the organization's goals.

CORPORATE STRATEGIC PLANNING

Long-run planning that incorporates defining the mission statement, establishing strategic business units, assigning resources to each SBU, planning new business.

COSTS, FIXED

All expenses that will remain the same no matter how many clients take a tour.

COSTS, TOTAL

The sum of the fixed and variable costs for any given level of production.

COSTS, VARIABLE

All expenses that change according to the number of clients who take a tour.

COUCHETTES

Sleeping accommodation provided by some European railroads, consisting of a day compartment which may be converted into bunks for four (1st class) or six (2nd class) passengers. Pillows and blankets are provided.

COUNSELLING

Counselling involves advising management about public issues and company positions and image.

COUNTRY OF COMMENCEMENT OF TRANSPORTATION (COC)

The country from which travel on the first international sector takes place.

COUNTRY OF PAYMENT

The country where payment is made by the purchaser to the TC Member or its Agent.

COUPONS

Documents issued by tour operators in exchange for which travellers receive pre paid accommodation, meals, sightseeing trips etc. Also referred as vouchers.

COUPON, ELECTRONIC

An electronic Flight Coupon or other value document held in Carrier's database.

COUPON, FLIGHT

That part of an airline ticket which contains details of the flight reserved for a passenger.

COUPON, PASSENGER

For carbonized documents: that portion of the Passenger Ticket and Baggage Check that constitutes the passenger's written evidence of the contract of carriage.

COURSE

Direction in which the ship is headed, usually expressed in compass degree.

CREW RESOURCE MANAGEMENT

Provides training to teach pilots, cabin crews and other airline personnel to work as a team to reduce errors. CRM training is now required of airlines around the world.

CREW

All ship's employees.

CROSS-SELLING

The strategy of purchasing new products to current customers based on their past purchases. Cross-slling is designed to widen the customer's reliance on the company and decreases the likelihood of the customer switching to a competitor.

CRUISE

An all expense prepaid tour pre-arranged by a luxury ship to a specific port.

CRUISE DIRECTOR

Individual responsible for overseeing the entertainment, public address announcements, and cruise programming staff on board a ship.

CULTURAL IMPACT

The effect of tourism activity or tourism development on the culture of the region or locality.

CULTURAL TOURISM

A form of tourism in which the culture and traditions of the region is the main attraction.

CULTURE ENVIRONMENT

Institutions and other forces that affect society's basic values, perceptions, preferences, and behaviours.

CULTURE

The set of basic values, perceptions, wants, and behaviours learned by a member of society from family and other important institutions.

CULTURE, ORGANIZATIONAL

The pattern of shared values and beliefs that gives members of an organization meaning and provides them with the rules for behaviour in that organization.

CURRENCY OF COUNTRY OF PAYMENT

The currency in which international fares from that country are denominated.

CUSTOMER CONTACT EMPLOYEES

Employees that come in direct contact with a customer.

CUSTOMER PORTFOLIO

A term used to denote the mix of customers. A particular service organization may target to ensure that all customer segments are desirable and compatible with one another.

CUSTOMER RELATIONSHIP MANAGEMENT

Activity directed towards developing long-term and committed customers. An overall marketing strategy aimed at keeping strong client commitment.

CUSTOMER SATISFACTION

Customer satisfaction with a purchase depends on the product's performance relative to a buyer's expectations. If performance matches expectations, the consumer is satisfied.

CUSTOMER SERVICE

All customer provider interactions other than proactive selling and the core product delivery that facilitate the organizations relationship with its customers.

CUSTOMS

A security check of a government, located at various entry points such as airports, seaports and border posts, in order to prevent illegal traffiking of goods and other items.

CUSTOMS

Authority in a country responsible for collecting taxes on imported merchandise or merchandise brought in from outside that country. This authority is also responsible for processing the flow or people, animals and goods including personal property and hazardous materials in and out of their country. They work to prevent smuggling and prevent forbidden goods from entering or leaving the country.

CYBERSPACE SETTING

Any Web site on the Internet, subject to all of the principles and concepts that apply to managing the tangible evidence of a conventional service environment.

CYCLE

Captures the medium-term wave movement of sales resulting from changes in the general economic and competitive activity.

COMPANION WAY

Stairway leading from the deck to passenger cabin areas.

CONSOLIDATORS

Based on some offshore markets, consolidators buy airfares in bulk from airlines and sell these to retail agents for on-sale to consumers.

CREW BAR

Crew area near the bilge where standards of conduct and appearance are relaxed, and sometimes forgotten.

CREW CABIN

Crew members are often berthed in separate quarters from the passengers. Accommodations depend on your position on board. Crew are expected to share cabins while officers are given single accommodations. Cabin stewards are assigned to crew and passengers areas in order to maintain fleet health and safety regulations. Crew cabins are small and used for little more than sleeping.

CREW SHORE LEAVE

Specific hours granted to crew members for going ashore.

CRUISE LINE INTERNATIONAL ORGANIZATION (CLIO)

An organization formed to promote cruising conduct educational programs on cruising for agency staff and management, and to provide a forum for discussion among cruise lines. Travel agencies may become associate members.

SECTION 2: D, E & F

Leisure travel, destination traffic, airlines, marketing, domestic traffic, sales and marketing, market research, e–ticketing, hotel meals, eco-tourism, air safety, eurorail, fare construction, flight schedule and miscellaneous.

DAMAGE

Includes death, injury, delay, loss, partial loss or other damage of whatsoever nature arising out of or in connection with carriage or other services performed by carrier incidental thereto.

DATA, PRIMARY

Information collected for specific purpose at hand.

DATA, SECONDARY

Information that already exists somewhere, having been collected for another purpose.

DATE LINE, INTERNATIONAL

Imaginary line are approximately 180° latitude in the Pacific Ocean where, by international agreement, the earth's day begins.

DATE OF TRANSACTION DAYS

The date of issuance of the ticket, MCO or PTA means full calendar days, including Sundays and legal holidays.

DATES, REVIEW

A periodic evaluation of the progress of the sale and promotion of a group combined with attendant cabin utilization.

DAY RATE

Special rate for the use of a room during the day from approx 0800 hours to 1800 hours.

DAY VISITOR

A tourist who does not stay overnight at the destination. Also known as an excursionist.

DAYLIGHT SAVING TIME

A particular time of the year in some regions in some countries of the world when clocks are set forward by one / two hours to extend the daylight into the evening hours.

DAYS

Full calendar days, including Sundays & legal holidays.

DEBARKATION

Exiting from the ship.

DECK CHAIR

Open deck chaise longue which is generally provided on a complementary basis.

DECK PLAN

An overhead diagram illustrating cabin and public room locations in relation to each other.

DECLINE STAGE

The product-life-cycle stage when a product's sales decline.

DECOMPRESSION

Loss or reduction of cabin pressure or altitude within the aircraft. (may be slow or rapid)

DELAMINATION

Occurs within composite materials, which consist of layers of fibres embedded in a resin matrix. When subjected to cyclic stress, the fibres may tear off the matrix and the layers of the material then separate from each other.

DELUXE ROOM

A regular size sleeping room in a hotel. This type of room would offer the best location, the best view and the highest level of comfort, furnishings, amenities and décor. Bedding usually includes a queen size or king size bed with comfortable mattresses.

DEMANDS

Human wants that are backed by buying power.

DEMAND CURVE

A curve that shows the number of units the market will buy in a given time period at different prices that might be char.

DEMOGRAPHIC SEGMENTATION

Dividing the market into groups based on demographic variables such as age, gender, family size, family life cycle, income, occupation, education, religion, race, and nationality.

DEMOGRAPHY

The study of human population in terms of size, density, age, sex, race occupation and other statistics.

DEMONSTRATE

To show how a product or service will meet the needs of potential client.

DEMONSTRATION EFFECT

Tendency for the local residents in the host areas to be influenced by the behaviour of the tourists and to imitate their mode of dress, food habits and even some of the cultural patterns etc.and assimilate it as their own.

DEPOSIT

Money sent to hold the reservation for a specific amount of time.

DEREGULATION

The process by which governments remove restrictions on business to encourage efficient operation of markets.

DESCENT

Downward path of an aircraft.

DESCRIPTIVE RESEARCH

Marketing research to better describe marketing problems, situations, or markets, such as the market potential for a product or the demographics and attitudes of consumers. It involves collecting data in order to test hypotheses or answer questions concerning the current status of the subject of the study. Data are typically collected through a questionnaire survey, an interview, or observation.

DESK, FRONT

Reception area in a hotel where guests check in and check out. This is the first contact point of guests with hotel employees.

DESTINATION FACILITIES

All plant and infrastructure available in a country, in area of local destination.

DESTINATION WEDDING PACKAGE

One of the fastest growing, and most lucrative products to sell are destination weddings which combine a wedding ceremony with a honeymoon, all in the same city, country or resort, at times including friends and family as guests.

DESTINATIONAL TOURIST

A tourist who terminates his journey at a particular country for the purpose of making a tour travelling from place to place for pleasure in that country.

DESTINATIONAL TRAFFIC

Persons (tourists) carried by transportation lines and terminating their journey at one particular place.

DESTINATIONS, MACRO

Destinations that contain thousands of micro destinations, including regions, states, cities, towns, and even visitor destinations within a town.

DESTINATION

The place at which traveller terminates his journey. It may also mean ultimate stopping place according to contract of carriage. It may also mean places with some form of actual or perceived boundaries such as physical boundary of an island, political boundaries or even market created boundaries.

DEVELOPMENT, SUSTAINABLE

A process of developing land, cities, business, and communities, that "meets the needs of the present without compromising the ability of future generations to meet their own needs".

DIFFERENTIATED MARKETING

A market-coverage strategy in which a firm decides to target several market segments and designs separate offers for each.

DIRECT FARE

For fare construction purposes, a fare between two points without the application of construction calculation.

DIRECT FLIGHT

A flight which does not require passengers to change the aircraft between starting point and destination. For example one can directly fly from Singapore to Los Angeles without changing an aircraft.

DIRECT MAIL

A form of promotion that involves the mailing of letters, flyers, postcards, brochures, questionnaires, newsletters or other printed materials to past, present and prospective clients.

DIRECT MARKETING

Marketing through various advertising media that interact directly with consumers, generally calling for the consumers to make a direct response.

DIRECT ROUTE FARE

The fare over the direct route between two points.

DIRECT ROUTE

The shortest all year route operated in both directions between ticketed points at which it exercises traffic rights.

DIRECT SALES METHOD

Selling direct to the end user with promotional efforts using advertising, direct mail or telephone sales.

DIRECT SALE

A marketing method used by principals to sell their products and services direct to the customer, instead of using agents. Although no commission is payable, their marketing and sales costs are generally higher, since every enquiry is dealt with their own staff.

DIRECT-MAIL MARKETING

Direct marketing through single mailing that include letters, ads, samples, foldouts, and other sales aids sent to prospects on mailing lists.

DIRECT-MARKETING CHANNEL

A marketing channel that has no intermediary levels.

DIRECTOR, CRUISE

Individual responsible for overseeing the entertainment, public address announcements, and cruise programming staff on board a ship.

DISCOUNT

A straight reduction in price on purchases during a stated period of time.

DISIMBARKATION

The leaving of an aircraft after landing, except by crew or passengers continuing on the next stage of the same through flight.

DISKS

Disks are devices that are used to store information.

DISPLAY

In general, whatever attracts.

DISTRIBUTION CHANNEL (MARKETING CHANNEL)

A set of interdependent organizations involved in the process of making a product or service available for use or consumption by a consumer or business user.

DISTRIBUTION CHANNEL

A set of independent organizations involved in the process of making a product or service available for use or consumption by a consumer or business user.

DIVING, CLIFF

Cliff diving is the act of diving from a high cliff into a river, lake or ocean below the cliff. It has been practiced as an unorganized activity both for recreation and other purposes. It is an sport, with large-scale competitions held in several places of the world. Cliff diving is classified as an extreme sport because of the inherent dangers.

DOCUMENT, STOLEN

An Accountable Traffic Document which is removed from the possession of its lawful custodian as a result of a break-in, burglary, robbery or theft, or which has been fraudulently obtained from a traffic document distributor.

DOMESTIC INDEPENDENT TRAVEL

A tour construed to meet the specific desire of a client within a single country.

DOMESTIC TOURISM

Tourism that does not entail outside the country's national boundaries by its citizen. This may include holidays, short breaks and business journeys.

DOMESTIC TOURIST

A local person who makes a tour travelling from place to place for pleasure, business, mission, family, meeting etc. within the country.

DOMESTIC, CARRIAGE

Carriage in which according to the contract of carriage, the place of departure, the place of destination or stopover and the entire transportation are within one nation or its territories.

DOUBLE

Room in a hotel with a double bed that can be used for either one or two people. It could also be a bed designed for two people.

DOWNGRADE

To be moved to a lower class of service. Sometimes happens when a smaller aircraft is used on a route normally served by a larger one, or in an overbooking situation.

DRAFT

Measurement in feet from waterline to lowest point of ship's keel.

DRAG

The force of air opposing the forward movement of the airplane.

DUTY FREE

Goods sold at ports or airports that are free of government taxes and customs duties. Some countries have allowances of how much duty free merchandise a person may bring back into their country. These restrictions usually apply to liquor, wine, tobacco, perfume, Jewellery and other gifts and souvenirs.

DUTY–FREE SHOPS

A shopping area with a number of shops located at air, sea and bus terminals selling goods which are exempted from local excise and are therefore lower in cost than available in the local market.These goods are sold to the bonafied passengers both arriving and departing having valid travel documents.

DYNAMIC PACKAGING

Websites mimic the experience of visiting a travel agent and negotiate a deal the consumer wants. Websites also allow the travel agent to package their own holidays and make better margins, while still offering a competitive price.

DECK DEPARTMENT

The deck department is responsible for maintaining, navigating, and engineering the ship. All ships, cruise or cargo, have the same deck position requirements.

DRAFT

Distance from the waterline to the bilge; large cruise liners have a draft of about 7 meters.

E-FREIGHT (EF)

A project designed to remove all the paper for all industry participants in air cargo transportation by 2010 by moving to an industry-wide, simpler, electronic and paper-free environment.

E-MAIL

Electronic mail is an electronic message sent via computer networks from one user to another.

E-TICKET

Electronic ticket is a digital form of a reservation. A passenger is issued a receipt from a machine or via email that contains a record locator or reservation number that confirms a booking or reservation. This information is available on the computer at the check-in counter and the passenger presents this confirmation number upon check in and is issued a boarding pass. It eliminates the need for a paper ticket. E tickets offer greater flexibility for airlines by eliminating manual tasks to process and account for paper tickets.

ECO –LODGE

Primarily located in remote and wild areas, these use very limited typical infrastructure elements and services found in more traditional settings such as access by paved highways, public transport services, electric and telephone lines, piped potable water, public drainage and sewage, refuse collection and disposal medical services, shopping, etc.

ECO-TOURISM

Eco-tourism is a purposeful travel to natural areas to understand the cultural and natural history of the environment, taking care not to alter the integrity of the ecosystem, whilst producing economic opportunities that make the conservation of natural resources financially beneficial to its local citizen.

"Environmentally responsible travel which involves visits to relatively undisturbed natural areas in order to enjoy and appreciate nature (any accompanying cultural feature both past and present) that promotes conservation, has low visit or impact and provides for active socio - economic involvement of local people."

ELECTRONIC COUPON

An electronic Flight Coupon or other value document held in Carrier's database.

ELECTRONIC MISCELLANEOUS DOCUMENT (EMD)

An electronic record issued by a carrier or its authorized agent, in accordance with applicable tariffs, for the issuance of the MCO or Tour Order.

ELECTRONIC SHOPPING

Direct marketing through a two- way system that links consumers with the seller's computerized catalogue by cable or telephone lines.

ELECTRONIC TICKETING (ET)

A new means of issuing tickets through electronic means (i.e., through the Internet and the use of self-service kiosks).

ELEVATOR

The hinged part of the horizontal stabilizer that is used to deflect the tail up and down.

EMBARKATION

The boarding of an aircraft for the purpose of commencing a flight except by such crew or passengers as have embarked on a previous stage in the same through flight.

EMIGRATION

Going out of the country to another country.

EMOTIONAL APPEALS

Message appeals that attempt to stir negative or positive emotions that will motivate purchase ; examples include fear, guilt, shame, love, humour, pride, and joy appeals.

EMPENNAGE

The tail assembly, which is the rear part of the airplane.

EMPLOYEES, CUSTOMER CONTACT

Employees that come in direct contact with a customer.

EMPOWERMENT

When a firm empowers employees, it moves the authority and responsibility to make decisions to the line employees from the supervisor.

END-ON COMBINATION

Combination of two or more fares which could be ticketed separately at a fare construction point (not applicable to local combination).

ENDORSEMENT

An authority from a carrier to transfer a transportation (document like ticket or flight coupons) to another carrier.

ENGLISH BREAKFAST

This type of breakfast is generally served in Great Britain. It usually includes hot or cold cereal, bacon or ham and eggs, toast, butter, jam or marmalade and beverage (though not juice).

ENROUTE

Along the way to a destination.

ENVIRO- FRIENDLY

Some hotels have designated certain rooms or floors to be environmentally friendly.

ENVIRONMENT IMPACT ASSESSMENT (EIA)

A set of procedures to assess in advance, the likely effects of tourism development project on the environment. It is a legal requirement in many countries such as USA and countries of European Union. Some of the coastal region also have these requirements.

ENVIRONMENT, CULTURE

Institutions and other forces that affect society's basic values, perceptions, preferences, and behaviours.

ENVIRONMENT, MACRO

The larger societal forces that affect the whole micro environment: competitive, demographic, economic, natural, technological, political, and cultural forces.

ENVIRONMENTAL FACTORS

Social, political, and economic factors that affect a firm and its marketing programme.

ENVIRONMENTAL IMPACT

Positive and negative effects of tourism on the natural and built attractions.

ENVIRONMENTAL MANAGEMENT PERSPECTIVE

A management perspective in which a firm takes aggressive actions to affect the publics and forces in its marketing environment rather than simply watching and reacting to it.

ENVIRONMENT

The total of the things or circumstances which surround us and may refer to the natural or built environment or some other set of conditions or influences like economic socio-cultural and political.

EQUIPMENT

The type of aircraft that an airline flies.

ESCORT

A professional tour escort often called Tour Manager or courier.

ESCORT TOUR

A tour accompanied by a professional Tour Escort also called Tour Manager.

ESTIMATED FLIGHT TIME

The overall general flight time between two points (the point of departure and the point of arrival).

ESTIMATED TIME OF ARRIVAL (ETA)

The time at which a flight is expected to arrive at the destination.

ESTIMATED TIME OF DEPARTURE (ETD)

The time at which a flight is projected to depart from a particular city.

EUROPEAN PLAN

Hotel accommodation with no meals whatsoever included in the cost of the tariff of the room.

EUROPEAN UNION (EU)

European Union is a family of democratic European Countries, committed to working together for peace and prosperity. It is not a state intended to replace existing states, but it is more than any other international organization. The EU is, in fact, unique. Its Member States have set up common institutions to which they delegate some of their sovereignty so that decisions on specific matters of joint interest can be made democratically at European level.

There are 25 members of EU including Austria, Belgium, Cyprus, Czech Republic, Denmark, Estonia, Finland, France, Greece, Hungary, Ireland, Italy, Latvia, Lithuania, Luxembourg, Poland, Malta, Portugal, Slovakia, Slovenia, Spain, Sweden, The Netherlands and the United Kingdom.

EURORAIL

Eurorail was established in 1959 as a way to organize Europe's large network of train and shipping companies into one large body. Prior to this point, travelling by train required purchasing tickets and paying for surcharges at each stop. The Eurail Group, created in 2001, is the main marketing and management sector of Eurail. It makes sure that Eurail travelling remains easy and open to all people.

Eurail's primary function is to make travelling easy and safe. It provides passes that allow travellers access to most railways, including some shipping lines. Prices are often set to fixed amounts. Eurail makes it easy for tourists to visit many different countries during a short period of time. This, along with the implementation of the Euro currency, creates a very accessible Europe.

A variety of passes are available that fit different kinds of travelling situations. Travellers can get passes that correlate with specific countries. Groups can purchase discounted passes, with the price depending on the size of the group.

Young travellers can purchase tickets with youth discounts and buy special unlimited travel packages. Most Eurail passes provide for free inner-city train transportation–though some private trains such as Eurostar, TGV and may require an additional fee.

The Eurail consists of 20 European countries, along with popular vacation spots such as France, Germany, Italy and Spain. Tourists can purchase a Eurail Select pass if they want to visit a specific group of bordering countries. Many of Europe's most historic and scenic rail lines are available through the Eurail pass. Some of the most beautiful routes include the Romsdal railway, the Oslo-Bergen railway, the Glacier Express, the West Highland Railway and the Venice Simplon Orient Express.

Eurail has helped to revive train transport in Europe. It has also helped to keep some of the older historic trains alive and running. Tourists now have additional incentive to see more of Europe rather than one or two countries. By creating a smooth network of shipping and domestic travelling, Eurail has helped the European economy expand.

EVACUATION

Emergency deplaning of passengers using all available exits.

EVALUATION, ALTERNATIVE

The stages of the buyer decision process in which a consumer uses information to evaluate alternative brands in the choice set.

EVENTS

Occurrences staged to communicate message to target audiences, such as news, conferences or grand openings.

EXCESS BAGGAGE

A passenger's baggage presented at check in counter of an airline that is in excess (either in terms of weight or dimensions) of free allowance on which charges are to be paid.

EXCESS, BAGGAGE

That part of the baggage, which is in excess of the free baggage allowance and for which the passenger has to pay extra freight charges.

EXCHANGE ORDER

A document issued by a carrier or its agents requesting issue of an appropriate ticket or provision of services to the person named in such document.

EXCHANGE VOUCHER

A document issued by a carrier or its agents requesting issue of an appropriate passenger ticket and baggage check or provision of services to the person name in such document.

EXCHANGE

The act of obtaining a desired object from someone by offering in return.

EXCLUSIVE DISTRIBUTION

Giving a limited number of dealers the exclusive right to distribute the company's products in their territories.

EXCURSION FARES

These fares are priced midway between APEX and full fare economy class. There are no advance booking requirements, but often a minimum stay abroad is mandatory. The passenger can change his booking and also stopover without surcharge. Different airlines however, have conditions on this.

EXCURSION FARES

Promotional fares usually for the round trip and for a specified period of time.

EXCURSIONIST

A temporary visitor staying less than twenty four hours in the country visited.

EXPECTED SERVICE

The service that customers feel they will receive from a service provider.

EXPERIMENTAL RESEARCH

The gathering of primary data by selecting matched groups of subjects, giving them different treatments, controlling related factors, and checking for differences in group responses. The researcher manipulates at least one independent variable (cause) and observes the effect on one or more dependent variables (effect).

EXPLORATORY RESEARCH

Marketing research to gather preliminary information that will help to better define problems and suggest hypotheses.

EXTENSIVE PROBLEM SOLVING

Buyer behaviour in cases in which buyers face complex buying decisions for more expensive, less frequently purchased products in an unfamiliar product class. Buyers engage in extensive information search and evaluation.

F & B OUTLETS

Another term used for eating and drinking establishments.

FACILITATION

The act of assisting progress or helping to move forward. To make easier or less difficult. Promoting any measures which will facilitate international travel with main emphasis on achieving minimum entry and exit formalities for temporary visitor.

FACILITIES

Services which enable tourists to enter and move around the country with the maximum of ease and the minimum of obstacles and to secure maximum enjoyment of their visit.

FACILITIES, DESTINATION

All plant and infrastructure available in a country, in area of local destination.

FACILITIES, AIR NAVIGATION

Any equipment, system, or manned unit which provides a pilot with information to enable him/her to reach the intended destination, safely and on-time.

FACTOR, LOAD

Total Revenue Passenger kilometers divided by total aircraft seat kilometers (ASKs).

FACTORS, ENVIRONMENTAL

Social, political, and economic factors that affect a firm and its marketing programme.

FAM TOUR (FAMILIARISATION TOUR)

An all inclusive complimentary trip offered to travel professionals to gain first–hand knowledge about the destination / attraction or any other service which the supplier may need to promote the product.

FAMILIARISATION TOUR

Familiarization visits bring international media and travel trade to a destination to experience products and regions first hand. These are educational trips and provide marketing tool for reaching out to travel professionals, journalists and trade delegates. The familiarization tours.provide first hand information and real life experiences of the tourism product to the intermediaries who form part of the distribution system as well as the opinion leaders like travel journalists, travel writers, film and television producers etc.

FAMILIARISATION VISIT

A visit made by a member of travel industry to a destination for the purpose of learning more about the destination and its features. These trips are informative and educational in nature and staff working in travel agencies, tour operators, airlines or tourist information office are encouraged to take them in order to keep themselves up-to-date with their product knowledge. These trips are usually funded by the organizations themselves and can form part of their general marketing strategy. These trips are also sponsored by National Tourism Organizations (NTO) as a marketing strategy to increase tourism in their countries.

FAMILIARIZATION TOURS

Discounted or complimentary tours are offered to travel agents or wholesalers to introduce them to a destination or product (also known as FAM trips). The cost of the Familiarization Tours is borne by company or a National Tourism Organization (NTO).

FAMILY LIFE CYCLE

The stages through which families might pass as they mature.

FAN TAIL

The rear or aft overhang of the ship.

FARE COMPONENT

A portion of an itinerary between two consecutive fare construction points.

FARE CONSTRUCTION POINTS

The terminal points of a fare component (these are also termed fare break points).

FARE, ADULT

The fare for a person who has attained his twelfth birthday.

FARE, APPLICABLE

For fare construction purposes, a fare which is established after the application of all fare construction calculations, e.g. excess mileage fare, higher intermediate fare, etc.

FARE, CABOTAGE

Special reduced fares known as "Cabotage Fares" are available but only to the nationals of the territories qualifying as Cabotage traffic.

FARE, CONSTRUCTED

Unspecified through fares created by the use of add-on amounts, or two or more fares shown as a single amount in a fare calculation.

FARE, CRUISE

The actual cost of the cruise excluding all extras such as taxes, port charges, airfare, gratuities and the like.

FARE, DIRECT

For fare construction purposes, a fare between two points without the application of construction calculation.

FARE, INFANT

The fare for a person who has not attained his second birthday.

FARE, SPECIAL

A fare other than the normal fare.

FARE, TOUR BASING

A reduced round trip fare available on specified dates, and between specified times, only to those passengers who purchase pre-planned, pre-paid tour arrangements from an agent prior to their departure.

FARES, EXCURSION

These fares are priced midway between APEX and full fare economy class. There are no advance booking requirements, but often a minimum stay abroad is mandatory. The passenger can change his booking and also stopover without surcharge. Different airlines however, have conditions on this.

FARE

The amount charged by the carrier for the carriage of a passenger and his allowable free baggage and is the current fare which an airline, normally uses and holds out to the public, or the appropriate segment of the public, as being applicable to the class of service to be furnished.

FAST FOOD OUTLETS

An outlet primarily serving hot ready-made food (snack) at a short notice. The outlets are very popular with tourists and these serve food quickly and at budget price. Most of the fast food outlets are part of well-known local or international chains.The outlets are generally located in metro cities and in commercial and tourist centres.

FATHOM

Measurement of distance equal to 6 feet.

FAX, BROADCAST

A method of promotion using a fax machine to deliver a message, letter, or advertisement to many people in a short period of time.

FEASIBILITY ANALYSIS

A detailed study of a project proposal to see whether the project is capable of being carried out and is practicable.

FEATURE

A characteristic or description of a product or service.

FEE, CANCELLATION

Penalty levied by airlines when a passenger fails to use a reservation.

FERRY

A vessel used to carry passengers, goods or vehicles across relatively short stretches of water. The vessel in many countries supplement the surface transport.

FIRST CARRIER

The participating carrier over whose air routes the first section of carriage under the ticket is taken or performed.

FIRST CLASS HOTEL

This establishment is of superior category where rooms are provided with telephone, private bathrooms and toilet. Restaurant and laundry services are also available.

FIRST CLASS

Symbolized by "F" in most airlines. Passengers travelling in this class are seated in a separate section with superior seating, a la carte menu and complimentary drinks. Passengers also get extra baggage allowance, unlimited stopovers and there are no cancellation charges.

FIRST SEATING

The earlier of two meal-times in the ship's dinning room.

FIT

Abbreviation for "foreign independent tour" which refers to a custom-designed tour.

FIXED CONVERSION RATE (FCR)

Irrevocable fixed exchange rate between the euro and the legacy currencies of EMU countries.

FIXED COSTS

All expenses that will remain the same no matter how many clients take a tour.

FLAPS

Flaps provide additional lift when needed and therefore have various degree settings. Flaps are hydraulically actuated and are used for take off and landing. Flaps are mounted on hinges on the trailing edge of the wing. Flaps are retracted in the climb phase and extended during the descent phase. Flaps are deployed downward on takeoff and landing to increase the amount of force produced by the wing.

FLIGHT COUPON

That part of an airline ticket which contains details of the flight reserved for a passenger.

FLIGHT CREW

Term referring to pilots.

FLIGHT DATA RECORDER

A device that records aircraft performance parameters. It is an aid to study air safety issues, material and jet performance and is also used in aircraft accident analysis.

FLIGHT DATA RECORDERS (FDRS)

Are referred to as " Black Boxes", the FDR onboard the aircraft records many different operating conditions of the flight. By regulation, the FDRs on newly manufactured aircraft must monitor at least 88 important parameters, such as time, altitude, airspeed, heading and aircraft altitude.

FLIGHT ENGINEER

Some types of aircraft have 3 pilots in the cockpit. Flight Engineer sits behind and to the right of the co-pilot and monitors all the aircraft systems. Many of today's modern jets do not have this position.

FLIGHT INFORMATION SERVICES

The Air Navigation Service that provided the information a pilot needs to decide whether a flight can continue safely.

FLIGHT NUMBER

An alphanumeric code, made up of a 2–character airline code plus between 1 and 4 numbers, assigned to a particular route.

FLIGHT NUMBER

Official number given to a commercial flight.

FLIGHT PATH

The direction of an aircraft in the air.

FLIGHT PLAN

Detailed document completed by the captain prior to every flight. It includes the planned routing, flying time, altitude and amount of fuel on board and an alternate airport if the plane is unable to land at the original destination airport.

FLIGHT RELEASE

A required verification by a qualified release officer that the flight meets certain requirements such as: the pilot in command is qualified, the passengers on board are legal to be on board, the specific airport and time frame in which the flight is to be operated. This information must be confirmed before the flight can operate.

FLIGHT SCHEDULE

The timetable showing all flights of an airline, and their scheduled departure and arrival times.

FLIGHT TIME, ESTIMATED

The overall general flight time between two points (the point of departure and the point of arrival).

FLIGHT, CHARTER

A flight operated by an airline whose aircraft has been hired or chartered by an individual or an organization. Travel agents and tour operators charter aircraft as a means of transporting their package tour clients to holiday (resort) destinations. The charters do not operate according to fixed schedule. Tourists are often prepared to accept this risk of uncertainty in exchange for lower prices for their holidays.

FLIGHT, CONNECTING

A flight which transfers a passenger to another aircraft in another city. It also means a flight that requires the passenger to change aircraft as part of the itinerary. An example would be of passenger travelling from New Delhi to New York via London. The passenger in this case will be required to change the aircraft at London to proceed to New York.

FLIGHT, DIRECT

A flight which does not require passengers to change the aircraft between starting point and destination. For example one can directly fly from Delhi to Chicago without changing an aircraft.

FLIGHTS, SCHEDULED

Typically take place using predetermined routes according to a planned timetable.

FLORA AND FAUNA

Flora refers to the plant life occurring in a particular region, generally the naturally occurring or indigenous plant life Fauna is all of the animal life of any particular region or time.

FLY / CRUISE TOUR

A travel plan wherein the travellers fly to a port of embarkation and then board a cruise ship for most of the tour. Fly cruise are generally part of the tour package.

FLY / DRIVE TOUR

An independent tour that allows travellers to visit multiple destinations during their trip and usually includes air transport, a car rental and lodging at several hotels.

FLY–CRUISE

Travel plan when in order to board a ship the travellers have to fly to the port of embarkation.

FOLDER

One piece of illustrated paper which can be folded in a number of folds containing information on a product. It is usually printed on a single sheet and then folded for easy handling.

FORECASTING

The art of estimating future demand by anticipating what buyers are likely to do under a given set of conditions.

FOREIGN INDEPENDENT TOUR (FIT)

This type of tour offered by travel agent / tour operators refers to custom designed tour taking into consideration the requirement of the tourist.

FORM, BOOKING

A form completed by a travel agent when a booking is created. The form records details of the customer's name, contact address and telephone number, itinerary, payment details, and booking conditions.

FORWARDING CARRIER

The carrier responsible for the condition which creates a need for involuntary change in the passenger's journey; on missed connections the carrier on whose flight a passenger is originally ticketed to be carried to a connection point.

FORWARD

Toward the fore or bow of the ship.

FRANCHISING

A continuing relationship in which the franchisor provides a licensed privilege to do business, plus assistance in organizing, merchandising and management in return for a consideration from the franchise.

FRANCHISE ORGANIZATION

A contractual vertical marketing system in which a channel member called a franchiser links several stages in the production distribution process.

FRANCHISE

A contractual association between a service organization (a franchiser) and independent business people (franchisees) who buy the right to own and operate one or more units in the franchise system.

FRAUDULENT /SUSPICIOUS DOCUMENT

An Accountable Traffic Documents that has been fraudulently altered or is otherwise suspicious and which the issuing airlines does not want honored.

FREE INDEPENDENT TRAVELLERS (FIT)

FIT's are visitors who travel around independently, as opposed to on coach or packaged tour.

FREEDOMS OF THE AIR

A set of commercial aviation rights granting a country's airline (S) the privilege to enter and land in another country's airspace; laid out in the Chicago Convention in 1944.

FREEDOMS OF THE AIR

Traffic rights bilaterally arranged between various nations.

FREIGHT FORWARDER

Combines small shipments from different shippers into larger shipments for economies of scale in the purchase of air transportation. The freight forwarder functions as a wholesaler of air transportation services, and includes specializations in traffic operations, customs clearances and shipping, and tariffs and schedules.

FREQUENCY

The number of times the average person in a target market is exposed to an advertising message during a given period.

FREQUENT GUEST PROGRAMME

Frequent guest programme in a hotel industry is similar to airline frequent flyer programme where guests accumulate points for using hotel services. The accumulated points then are redeemed towards upgrades, discounts and complimentary services and they also often linked to specific airline programmes.

FRONT DESK

Reception area in a hotel where guests check in and check out. This is the first contact point of guests with hotel employees.

FRONT OF THE HOUSE

The area of the hotel accessible to the public.

FRONT OFFICE

Part of the hotel that includes the Reception Desk, Hall Porter or Concierge or Guest Service Desk, Property Reservations and Bell or Porter Services.

FULL BOARD

Daily hotel rates which includes guest accommodation plus three meals.

FUNICARS

A mode of transport for tourists to travel over steep hill slopes. Funicars travel on the ground and are pulled by cable on the surface of a slope.

FUNNEL

The smokestack or chimney of the ship.

FUSELAGE

The body of the airplane, which extends from the nose to the tail. Most have a tube like shape and are covered with a lightweight aluminium skin. The fuselage houses the controls, crew, passengers, and cargo.

FORE AND AFT

Respectively, the front and back of the ship; together they refer to the entire ship.

FREE BOARD

Distance from the waterline to the deck.

SECTION 3: G, H, I & J

Group travel, global distribution system, hospitality, global positioning system, supplementary accommodation, itinerary, iata, ticketing, advertising, inbound travel, jet lag and miscellaneous.

G8 GROUP OF EIGHT

It refers to US, Japan, Germany, France, the UK, Italy, Canada and Russia. Formally known as the G7 before Russia officially joined in June 2002. The G8 is the most influential group of developed countries in terms of its role in the setting policy in the international financial system.

GALLEY

The area on the aircraft where food and beverages are stored and prepared.

GALLEY

Food preparation area.

GANGWAY

The placement of a platform or ramp at a gap in the gunwale or life lines for embarkation and disembarkation to a dock or tender. Gangways are used for convenience and security. Boarding or leaving the vessel by a means other than the gangway, without approval from the bridge, is a criminal offence.

GARNI HOTEL

These are establishments which do not have a restaurant facilities. Such hotels however, serve continental breakfast to their guests.

GARNI

When appended to the name of an hotel, this means that the establishment does not have a restaurant or dining room. Such hotels usually have a breakfast room.

GATE

The exit in the departure lounge that leads to the aircraft.

GATEWAY CITY

City airport serving the passenger as an entry or departure point in a foreign country.

GATEWAY

First point of arrival / last point of departure in a country / area.

GATEWAY

A major airport, seaport, rail or bus centre through which tourists and travellers enter from outside the region.

GEAR, LANDING

The undercarriage of an airplane, which consists of the wheels (or floats) upon which it moves when on the ground (or in the water).

The landing gear also supports the weight of the plane on the ground or in the water.

GEEK HOTEL

A geek hotel is for those who suffer from technophilia. The hotel is fitted out with gizmos and gadgets, rooms are Wi-Fi enabled, computers packed with software like photo, video and sound editing, cameras, wireless so that the geeky sort enjoys his/her holiday without missing out on the digital life. Those who wish to work on holiday can wish to do so.In many hotels, the décor too gives a technical feel.

GENERAL AVIATION

That segment of civil aviation that excludes air carriers.

GENERAL SALES AGENTS (GSA)

General sales agents are appointed by an airlines or any other organization in a particular territory to handle their bookings, inquiries, etc.

GEO TOURISM

Tourism that sustains or enhances the geographical character of the place–it's environment, culture, aesthetics, heritage, and the well being of its residents.

GEOGRAPHIC SEGMENTATION

Dividing a market into different geographical units such as nations, regions, countries, cities.

GEYSER

Jet of streaming water that shoots into the air, sometimes at a fairly regular intervals.

GIT

Group inclusive tour.

GLACIER

A frozen river of ice that moves slowly from areas of higher elevation to areas of lower elevations.

GLOBAL DISTRIBUTION SYSTEM (GDS)

The mean by which airlines offer for sale (distribute) their seats through computer terminals situated in travel and other airline offices throughout the world. Often referred to as computer reservation systems. Users may access a number of intermediary host systems to reserve airline seats, book car hire, or hotel accommodation. Several airlines have grouped together to form the host systems such as Amadeus, Galileo, Sabre, Apollo and Worldspan.

GLOBAL INDICATOR

The global routing applicable to fares.

GLOBAL POSITIONING SYSTEM (GPS)

The use of satellites to convey the positions of airplanes to air traffic controllers.

GO-SHOW

A passenger who shows up for a flight without a reservation.

GOVERNMENT RATE

A specially negotiated rate between a specific governmental agency and the hotel for qualified government employees.

GRAND TOURIST

A tour of the continent Europe formerly taken by young people. The development of the Grand Tour followed the shift in the focus on culture, and of economic and political power. The wealthy and educated from the states whose position of dominance in the world was comparatively new, visited countries that had passed their peak of prestige but were still venerated for historical and cultural reasons. The Grand Tour respected the learning antiquities and social refinements of the old world.

GRAND TOUR

The grand tour referred to a tour of the principal cities and places of interest in Europe, the focus on the tour being enrichment of the culture. The tour was influenced by European Renaissance, a great cultural movement that began in Italy in early 1300 AD and spread to England, France, Spain, Germany and many other countries and ended about 1600 AD. The Renaissance was a period of change and revival of Greek and Roman cultures. The famous works of art of Italian artists like Leonardo da Vinci, Michelangelo and Raphael inspired the Grand Tour. The younger generation from rich and aristocrat background undertook the Grand Tour which in addition to learning also included pleasure element.

GRATITUDES

The passenger's personal expression of thanks to the ship's service personnel for services received.

GRATUITIES

The passenger's personal expression of thanks (tips) to the ship's service personnel for services received.

GRAVITY

The natural force that tend to pull an airplane to the earth when in flight.

GREENPEACE

A non-governmental environmental organization with offices in over 41 countries and headquarters in Amsterdam, Netherlands. Greenpeace states its goal as to "ensure the ability of the earth to nurture life in all its diversity" Greenpeace uses direct action, lobbying and research to achieve its goals. The global organization states that it does not accept funding from governments, corporations or political parties, relying on individual supporters and foundation grants.

Greenpeace evolved from the peace movement and anti-nuclear protests in Vancouver, British Columbia in the early 1970's. On September 15, 1971, the newly found Don't Make a Wave Committee sent a chartered ship, Phyllis Cormack, renamed Greenpeace for the protest, from Vancouver to oppose United States testing of nuclear devices in Amchitka, Alaska, launching the first campaign of the organization and prompting the Don't Make a Wave Committee to adopt the name Greenpeace. In a few years Greenpeace spread to several countries and started to campaign on other environmental issues such as commercial whaling and toxic waste. In the late 1970's the different regional Greenpeace groups formed Greenpeace International to oversee the goals and operations of the regional organizations globally. Greenpeace received international attention during the 80's when the French intelligence agency bombed the flagship of Greenpeace, killing one. In the following years Greenpeace evolved into one of the largest environmental organizations in the world.

Today Greenpeace focuses on world wide issues such as global warming, deforestation, overfishing and nuclear power. Greenpeace is known for its direct actions and has been described as the most visible environmental organization in the world. Campaigns of Greenpeace have raised environmental issues to public knowledge and influenced both the private and the public sector.

GROSS DOMESTIC PRODUCT (GDP)

It is the total market value of all the final goods and services produced in a country over a period of one year.

GROSS DOMESTIC PRODUCT

The total value of all the goods and services produced within the borders of a nation during a specified period – usually a year.

GROSS REGISTERED TON (GRT)

A measurement of 100 cubic feet of enclosed revenue earning space within a ship.

GROUND HANDLERS

Ground handlers are agents who work on behalf of tour operators, travel agents, and principals and look after all arrangements once the group of tourists reach the destination. They facilitate the group's visit as per the programme.

GROUND ARRANGEMENTS

All services for the traveller by the tour operator after the traveller reaches his first foreign destination. Also required to as land arrangements.

GROUND SPEED

This is the speed of the aircraft in relation to the ground, which is the sum of the airplanes actual airspeed plus or minus the wind speed and current weather conditions.

GROUND TIME

Period of time an aircraft and /or crew spend on the ground between flights.

GROUP BOOKINGS

A set of rooms set-aside for groups of ten or more people and negotiated at special price. This negotiated price is lower than the normal price.

GROUP FARES

Discounted fares for the groups of 14 or more individuals. As per the IATA guidelines, one ticket is given free to a escort travelling with the group.

GROUP INCLUSIVE TOUR (GIT)

A tour which includes air and ground arrangements for a minimum of 15 persons. They may or may not stay together as a group for both the land and air portion of the trip.

GROUP, AFFINITY

A group bound together by common interest or affinity. Where charters are concerned, this common bound makes the concerned members eligible for charter flights. The group must travel together on the departure and return flights but can travel independently where ground arrangements are concerned.

GROUP, ASPIRATIONAL

A group to which a person wishes to belong.

GROWTH STAGE

The product-life-cycle stage when a new product's sales start climbing quickly.

GROWTH/SHARE MATRIX

A model developed by the Boston Consulting Group to assist managers to plan business portfolios.

GUARANTEE SHARE

Acceptance by some lines of a single booking at the double-occupancy rate-thereby offering a saving in cost value-with the understanding that the client is willing to share use of the cabin with a stranger of the same sex.

GUARANTEED PAYMENT RESERVATION

Payment for a room is guaranteed and will be paid for by a company or organization whether it is used or not.

GUARANTEED TOUR

A tour which is guaranteed to operate unless cancelled 60 days prior to departure. In the event of cancellation within 60 days of the departure date, full commission is paid to agents of sold clients.

GUARANTEE

Hold status of reservation prepaid either by a cash deposit or credit / debit card number.

GUIDE

A person who is licensed to take paying guests on local sightseeing excursions.

GUIDED TOUR

A tour conducted only by local city guides.

GULF

A large area of an ocean that penetrates into land.

GV 10

This is a group ticket for 10 people travelling together. A discount fare originally created for tour operators. It is now widely used by airlines to conceal discounting to individual.

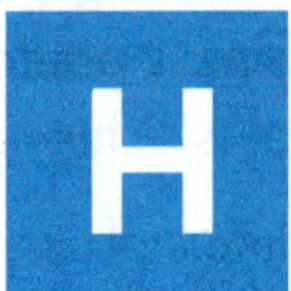

HALF BOARD

Includes two full meals per day; also known as MAP (Modified American Plan) as part of the price of a hotel room.

HALF PENSION

Hotel accommodation which includes continental breakfast and either table d'hote lunch or dinner in the price of the room. Also referred to as "Modified American Plan".

HALF ROUND TRIP FARE

Half of a specified or constructed round trip normal or special fare. In the absence of a specified or constructed round trip normal fare, the one way normal fare is considered to be a half round trip normal fare.

HALL PORTER

A hotel staff member who usually supervises luggage handling but may also perform the services of a concierge.

HALL PORTER'S DESK

Desk also called bell stand a portion of the lobby set aside for receiving luggage and distributing it to the guests in the rooms.

HANDICAPPED FACILITIES

Special equipment or room configurations that can accommodate wheelchair-bound or other disabled guests.

HANG GLIDING

A hang glider uses a semi-rigid wing made of fabric supported by a light alloy fern. It essentially flies like a glider where the directional control is achieved by of shift in glider's weight by the pilot.

HARDWARE

The electronic and mechanical components of a computer.

HEALTH CLUB

Health club in a hotel can include fitness rooms, sauna, swimming pool, Jacuzzi.

HEALTH SPA

A place of business with equipment and facilities for exercising and improving physical fitness

HEALTH TOURISM

It is a movement of tourists into a country for the consumption of health related services in the host country.

HERITAGE PROPERTIES

Properties which were built some generations ago and provide tangible links between the past, present and future and are based on the culture and history of the natural and built environment.

HERITAGE TOURISM

Tourism that respects natural and build environments, in short the heritage of the people and place, is called heritage tourism. Renewed appreciation for historical milestones, the development of "heritage traits" linking cultural landmarks, produce new tourism services and products that can assist local economies.

HERITAGE WALKS

A new trend becoming popular in different countries.These walks are eco- friendly covering places of cultural and natural interests. A guided heritage walk is to study the history of the area which is reflected in the architecture, crafts, culture and way of living of the people untouched by modernization and urbanization.The walks also provide an opportunity to the tourists to interact with local community.

HIGH SEASON

Time of year when tourist traffic and rates are usually the highest because demand is highest.

HISTORICAL RESEARCH

The studying, understanding, and explaining of past events. The purpose of historical research is to arrive at conclusions concerning causes, effects, or trends of past occurrences that may help explain present events and anticipate future events.

HOLD

Interior space(s) below the main deck for storing cargo.

HORIZONTAL DIVERSIFICATION STRATEGY

A product growth strategy whereby a company looks for new products that could appeal to current customers, which are technologically unrelated to its current line.

HORIZONTAL INTEGRATION

A growth strategy by which companies acquire competitors.

HORIZONTAL SEPARATION

The action undertaken by air traffic controllers requiring aircraft to operate at different positions in order to avoid collisions. Longitudinal separation requires the spacing between the estimated positions of the aircraft being separated to be never less than a prescribed minimum. Another form of horizontal separation is lateral separation. This ensures that the distance between those portions of the routes for which the aircraft are to be laterally separated is never less than an established distance to account for navigational inaccuracies plus a specified buffer.

HOSPICES

A shelter for the travellers maintained by the monks providing simple basic facilities.

HOSPITALITY INDUSTRY

Made up of those businesses that do one or more of the following: provide accommodation for the traveller, prepared food and beverage service, and entertainment for the traveller.

HOSPITALITY SUITE

A sitting room used to entertain client or guests. The facility usually has a sleeping room connected by a common door and includes bathroom facilities in both rooms.

HOST COMMUNITY

A community living permanently in a region / area which happens to be tourist destination and receive visitors as guests. The guests are temporary visitors who have come to enjoy tourist attractions.

HOSTED TOUR

A tour where participants have an opportunity to travel independently, but also to receive guidance and assistance from a host at each of the tour's destinations.

HOSTEL, YOUTH

A building which offers clean simple and inexpensive shelter to young people exploring their own country or the world travelling independently or in a groups for holiday or educational purpose.

HOTEL CHAINS

A group of hotels belonging to a major company and providing the same level of services in terms of accommodation and catering under a common brand name. The hotels may be located in various cities in a country or a region.

HOTEL VOUCHER

A coupon issued by a tour operator or a travel agent to the tourists, which covers prepaid elements of a trip like accommodation and meals. On arrival at the hotel, the client has to hand over the coupon to the representative of the hotel. The hotel later claims the payment from the issuing authority.

HOTEL, APARTMENT

A hotel containing apartments as well as accommodations for transients.

HOTEL, COMMERCIAL

Establishment catering to individuals on business and for tourists staying for a short time. The hotel provides a comfortable sleeping accommodation and meal services, ranging from modest rooms and a coffee shop to elegant suites and a first class specialty restaurant. This also includes additional facilities such as conference room, a banquet hall, business centre, etc. In big cities these hotels are generally located near the business districts or in the centre of the city.

HOTEL, RESORT

In addition to the facilities provided in the city hotels, resort hotels provide attractions such as swimming pools, private beaches, sport facilities like tennis courts and other outdoor and indoor recreational facilities. Resort hotels are situated in areas of scenic beauty, sightseeing attractions or in the surroundings providing entertainment opportunities. These could be of various types like beach resorts, health resorts, winter resorts etc.

HOTEL

An establishment which provides board and lodging for periods of time for those who may reserve their accommodation either in advance or on arrival at premises and who being able and ready to pay for their board and lodging and entertainment.

HOTELIER

A person, firm or corporation which provides hotel accommodation and / or meals refreshments etc. to visitors.

HOUSE KEEPING

The department in a hotel that is responsible for cleaning, tiding up and maintaining the sleeping rooms in the hotel.

HUB (HUB AND SPOKE)

An airline network concept, prompted by economic deregulation, whereby small aircraft carry passengers between small airports (feeders) and main airports (hubs). From there, passengers connect to large aircraft to fly the longer part of their journey. It increases air transportation efficiency by providing the right aircraft size and flight frequency for the right trip length and passenger volumes. It draws its name from its graphic shape.

HUB AND SPOKE

Air carriers use of selected cities as "hubs" or connected points for service on their systems to regional destinations.

HUB

An airport or city which serves as a central connecting point for aircraft, trains or buses outside feeder airports or cities.

HUMAN FACTORS

The study of how people interact with procedures, operating controls, tools and other products; can also be referred to as "ergonomics".

HYDROFOIL

A vessel raised partially above the surface of the water using fins and foils. It glides on the surface of the water very fast as there is no friction and drag caused by immersion in water.

IATA RATE OF EXCHANGE (OR IROE)

Rates of exchange notified by IATA to convert local currency fare to NUC and to convert total NUC amounts to the currency of the country of commencement of transportation.

IATA'OPERATIONAL SAFETY AUDIT (IOSA) PROGRAMME

An internationally recognized and accepted evaluation system designed to assess the operational management and control systems of an airline.

IMAGE, BRAND

The set of beliefs consumers hold about a particular branded product.

IMMEDIATE FAMILY

Includes spouse, children, parents, brothers, sisters, dependent relatives or dependents in the household.

IMMIGRATION

Official point of entry to a country, where the visas and passports of crew and passengers are checked.

IMMIGRATION AUTHORITY

Agency that monitors persons entering or leaving the country by validating appropriate documentation to allow entry to the country or to forbid entry to the country. The immigration authority has the right to forbid entry into the country because of missing documentation or because the person is a possible threat. In some countries Immigration is a separate agency from Customs.

IMPACT, CULTURAL

The effect of tourism activity or tourism development on the culture of the region or locality.

IMPACT, ENVIRONMENTAL

Positive and negative effects of tourism on the natural and built attractions.

IMPACTS, SOCIO CULTURAL

The impacts or effects of tourism on the social and cultural traditions of the host community. The impacts may both be positive or negative, good or bad depending upon the management of a destination.

IMPORT

To transfer data from one programme to another.

IN TRANSIT VISITOR

Person who interrupts a journey for a short period (less than 24 hours) either out of necessity or by choice without the transit lounge and not proceeding through Immigration and Customs.

IN-ROOM DINING

Food and beverage served in the sleeping rooms (also known as Room Service).

INBOUND TOUR OPERATOR

Inbound tour operators are responsible for preparing itineraries and booking the ground arrangements on behalf of internationally based wholesalers.

INBOUND TOURISM

From the point of view of a destination, this describes the tourists who arrive from another country. It is therefore, a form of international tourism contributing to the economy of the receiving nation.

INBOUND TRAVEL (INTERNATIONAL)

International inbound tourists (overnight visitors) are the number of tourists who travel to a country other than that in which they have their usual residence but outside their usual environment for a period not exceeding 12 months (some countries may have different rules for stay) and whose main purpose in visiting is other than an activity remunerated from within the country visited.

INBOUND TRAVEL

Inbound travel comprises short term arrivals into a country by nationals / residents of other countries.

INCENTIVE

A reward participants receive for achieving or exceeding a goal.

INCENTIVE TRAVEL

Travel and tourism products such as all-inclusive holidays given as reward to the employees for achievement or incentive to reach targets in business.

INCIDENT, AVIATION

An occurrence other than an accident, associated with the operation of an aircraft, which affects or could affect the safety of operations.

INCLUSIVE TOUR

A prearranged combination of air transportation and surface arrangements other than solely public transportation.

INCOME SEGMENTATION

Dividing the market into different income groups.

INDEPENDENT HOTEL

A hotel property not affiliated with any chain or group.

INDEPENDENT TOUR

A tour where participants travel independently without an accompanying group or tour guide.

INDEPENDENT TRAVEL, DOMESTIC

A tour construed to meet the specific desire of a client within a single country.

INDIRECT ROUTE

Any scheduled continuous air route other than a direct route.

INDUSTRY RATES

Rate for employees within the travel industry including those of airlines, hotels, travel agencies, tour operators, wholesale packagers.

INDUSTRY

The set of the sellers of a product.

INDUSTRY, AIR TRANSPORT

The area of commerce that uses aircraft for the transport of people and cargo. This applies to flights of government-certified companies that offer services to the public and for general aviation, which applies to private aircraft used for business or recreation.

INDUSTRY, AVIATION

The range of activities involved in building and flying aircraft. These include aircraft manufacturing, airport operations, and aviation support industries.

INDUSTRY, HOSPITALITY

Made up of those businesses that do one or more of the following: provide accommodation for the traveller, prepare food and beverage service, and entertainment for the traveller.

INFLUENCE, BUYING

Either an individual or a group within a category that has a decision-making role in a large-account sale.

INFORMATION SEARCH

The stage of the buyer decision process in which a consumer is aroused to search for more information; the consumer may simply have heightened attention or may go into active information search.

INFORMATIVE ADVERTISING

Advertising used to inform consumers about a new product or feature and to build primary demand.

INFRASTRUCTURE TOURISM

The basic essentials for tourism. Facilities such as access (roads, ports, airports), public services, such as water, electricity or sewerage and any service or facility that is needed before any tourism development can begin. In most of the cases funded by governments or a combination of public and private organizations.

INFRASTRUCTURE

The network of basic public services including communication and utility services such as roads, drains electricity, water, gas, sewage lines needed to support the development of land and putting up of superstructures.

INITIATOR

The person who first suggests or thinks of the idea of buying a particular product or services.

INNS

Inns are generally establishments or buildings where travellers can seek lodging, and usually food and drink. They are typically located in the country or along a highway.

Found in Europe, they possibly first sprang up when the Romans built their system of Roman roads two millennia ago. Some inns in Europe are several centuries old. In addition to providing for the needs of travellers, inns traditionally acted as community gathering places.

In Europe, it is the provision of accommodation, if anything, that now differentiates inns from taverns. The latter tend to supply alcohol (and, in the UK, usually soft drinks and sometimes food), but less commonly accommodation. Inns tend to be grander and more long-lived establishments; historically they provided not only food and lodging, but also stabling and fodder for the traveller's horse(s) and for horses for the mail coach.

INSIDE CABIN

A cabin having no windows or portholes to offer a view of the sea or river.

INSTRUMENT FLIGHT RULE (IFR)

A set of regulations and procedures for flying aircraft without the assumption that pilots will be able to see and avoid obstacles, terrain and other air traffic.

INSTRUMENT LANDING SYSTEMS (ILS)

A landing navigation system that is used only within a short distance from the airport. Its purpose is to help the pilot land the airplane. It is generally used only when visibility is limited and the pilot cannot see the airport and runway. An ILS consists of two independent sub-systems, one providing lateral guidance, the other vertical guidance to aircraft approaching a runway. The system, which is ground-based, broadcasts very precise directional signals.

INTANGIBILITY

A fundamental characteristic of services referring to the fact that a service cannot be seen, touched, held or put on a shelf 'because' it lacks a physical existence or form.

INTANGIBLE PRODUCT

A service that cannot be touched.

INTANGIBLE

Something without physical properties, incapable of being seen, tasted, felt, heard, or smelled. A service is intangible.

INTEGRATED DIRECT MARKETING

Direct-marketing campaigns that use multiple vehicles and multiple stages to improve response rates and profits.

INTEGRATION, BACKWARD

A growth strategy by which companies acquire businesses that supply them with products or services, such as restaurant chain purchasing a bakery.

INTEGRATION, HORIZONTAL

A growth strategy by which companies acquire competitors.

INTERACTIVE MARKETING

Marketing by a service firm to train effectively and motivate its customer-contact employees and all those who depend heavily on the quality of buyer-seller interaction.

INTERFACE

A pictorial representation on a computer screen of the files, data and programmes stored on the computer.

INTERLINE AGREEMENTS

Agreements between two or more transportation lines for the mutual benefit of the both.

INTERLINE TRANSFER

Transfer from the service of one carrier to the service of another carrier.

INTERLINE

When a passenger travels and connects to a different airline to reach a destination.

INTERMEDIARIES, MARKETING

Firms that help the company to promote, sell, and distribute its goods to final buyers; they include middlemen, physical distribution firms, marketing-service agencies, and financial intermediaries.

INTERMEDIATE CLASS

A class of service with seating standards which may be superior to those provided on economy/ tourist class but less liberal than standards provided in first class; provided that the intermediate class seat pitch shall not exceed 41 inches.

INTERMEDIATE STOP (TRANSIT)

Any city where a flight stops between its originating and terminating points.

INTERNAL ENVIRONMENTAL ANALYSIS

A periodical evaluation of company's strengths and weakness.

INTERNAL MARKETING

The policy of treating employees as internal customers of the organization, responding to employees needs or wants and promoting the organization and its policies to the employees.

INTERNATION SALE INDICATOR (ISI)

Transaction code such as SITS, SOTI, SITO, SOTO which help determine the fare construction checks to apply.

INTERNATIONAL AIR TRANSPORT ASSOCIATION (IATA)

IATA is an international industry trade group of airlines headquartered in Montreal, Quebec, Canada, where the International Civil Aviation Organization is also headquartered. IATA's mission is to represent, lead, and serve the airline industry. IATA represents some 230 airlines comprising 93% of scheduled international air traffic. Currently, IATA is present in over 150 countries. IATA was formed in April 1945, in Havana, Cuba. It is the successor to the International Air Traffic Association, founded in The Hague in 1919, the year of the world's first international scheduled services. At its founding, IATA had 57 members from 31 nations, mostly in Europe and North America. Today it has about 230 members from more than 140 nations in every part of the world.

The principal objective of IATA is to promote safe, regular and economical air transport for the benefit of the travelling population across the world and to foster air commerce. It is also to provide means for collaboration among the air transport enterprises engaged directly or indirectly in international air transport service.

INTERNATIONAL CIVIL AVIATION ORGANIZATION (ICAO)

An agency of the United Nations which sets international standards in such fields as air navigational facilities, air operations, airports, airworthiness of aircraft, and communications. In addition, the ICAO defines the protocols for air accident investigation followed by transport safety authorities in countries signatory to the Convention on International Civil Aviation, commonly known as the Chicago Convention. Its headquarters are located in Montreal, Canada.ICAO was formally established on April, 4, 1947 as a specialized agency of the United Nations.

INTERNATIONAL CIVIL AVIATION ORGANIZATION (ICAO)

The ICAO C ouncil adopts standards and recommended practices concerning air navigation, its infrastructure, flight inspection, prevention of unlawful interference, and facilitation of border-crossing procedures for international civil aviation. In addition, the ICAO defines the protocols for air accident investigation followed by transport safety authorities in countries signatory to the Convention on International Civil Aviation, commonly known as the Chicago Convention.

INTERNATIONAL DATE LINE

Imaginary line are approximately 180° latitude in the Pacific Ocean where, by international agreement, the earth's day begins.

The international Date Line is the imaginary line running from North Pole to South Pole through the Pacific Ocean, with the date differing in the east and the west, the east of the line being one day earlier. For example, if it is 27th May in USA, it will be 28th May in India.

INTERNATIONAL TRANSFER

A change from the International service of one carrier to another international service of the same carrier (online transfer) or to the international service of another carrier (International transfer).

INTERNATIONAL, CARRIAGE

Carriage in which according to the contract of carriage,

the place of departure, and any place of landing are situated in more than one nation. As used in this definition, the term national includes all territory subject to the sovereignty, mandate, authority or trust-ship thereof.

INTERNATIONAL HOTEL AND RESTAURANT ASSOCIATION (IH & RA)

IH & RA is an international trade association representing the interests of the hotel & restaurant industry. It was founded in the year 1949 and it's headquarters are located in Paris, France. IH & RA members are national hotel & restaurant associations through the world and international and national hotel & restaurant chains representing about 50 brands, officially recognized by the United Nations, IH & RA monitors and lobbies international agencies on behalf of the industry.

INTERNET

Global computer network that links computers via communication lines such as television cables, telephone lines or wireless connections.

The Internet is a worldwide network of computer networks linked to each other via telecommunication links.

INTRODUCTION STAGE

The product life cycle stage when a new product is first distributed and made available for purchase.

ISLAND TOURISM

Island Tourism is associated with a quite holiday in a island which gives feeling of remoteness or seclusion.

ISSUING AIRLINE

TC Member whose tickets are issued to the passengers.

ISSUING CARRIER

Airline whose ticket is issued or in whose name a ticket is issued.

ITINERARY, SUGGESTED

A preliminary itinerary provided by tour operators for the travellers consideration. This itinerary generally shows routing and approximate times as well as recommended hotels and suggested sight-seeing excursions, and spells out the conditions under which these services will be provided.

ITINERARY

A tourist itinerary is a composition of series of operations that are a result of the study of the market. A tourist itinerary follows a set pattern and there is no scope for deviation. A paper document is issued to customers with flight reservations and all booked flight details.

ITX

"Independent Inclusive Tour Excursion" fares. This is available to the public ostensibly, only as a component of holiday package which also includes hotel accommodation and / or car hire.

JAPANESE STYLE BEDDING

Bedding is stored out of sight during daytime and rolled out on the floor for sleeping.

JET LAG

Period of adjustments of biological rhythm after moving from one time zone to another, experienced as fatigue and lowered efficiency. It reflects the delay in synchronization of changes in the level of blood cortisol, the major steroid produced by the aderenal cortex, tummy bugs and the sun.

JET STREAM

A narrow band of very high-speed winds, usually found at altitudes between 20,000 and 40,000 feet. These winds usually blow from west to east and can reach speeds as high 200 miles per hour.

JETFOIL

A high-speed ferry powered by jet engines.

JETWAY (JETTY)

Enclosed tunnel like passage way brought to the aircraft that allows entry and exit from the aircraft.

JOINT AGENT

A person having authority to transact business for two or more transportation lines.

JOMBO JETS

These are the largest airlines, which are wide-body jets with fuselage diameter of 5 to 6 metres (16 to 20 ft). These aircrafts are frequently called twin-aisle running from the front to the back of the passenger cabin. Typical wide-body aircraft can accommodate between 200 to 600 passengers, who are usually seated 7 to 10 abreast.

JOURNEY

Travel or passage from one place to another. Completing a travel to the destination as per the ticket issued.

JUMP SEAT

A jump seat, officially known as an auxiliary crew station, is a seat in the cockpit for individuals not operating the aircraft. The term is also used as to refer to crew seat in the cabin, which are occupied by a flight attendant or other cabin crew during take off and landing. The cabin jump seats are typically located next to or near emergency exits so that flight attendance can quickly open the exit during an evacuation.

JUMPING, BUNGEE

This requires no equipment other than bungee chord made of nylon fibre of enough elasticity to be able to absorb the shock at the end of the jump. The only infrastructure required is a bridge or any structure which offers few hundred feet of free fall.

JUNIOR SUITE

A large room with two sections for sleeping and sitting. It usually includes a couch, coffee table and side chairs.

SECTION 4: K, L & M

Travel geography, leisure travel, aircraft, low cost carrier, long haul travel, miscellaneous charge order, tourism marketing, marketing concepts, motivation, market segments, marketing management, marketing research, media impacts, management information systems, and miscellaneous.

KEY ACCOUNTS

The most important accounts by sales volume / margin.

KEYBOARD

A keyboard is a device used to enter information and give instructions to the computer.

KING SIZE BED

Largest size double bed.

L

CARRIERS, LOW COST

Also known as "no-frills" airlines which offer generally low fares in exchange for eliminating many traditional passenger services.

LAGOON

Shallow body of water, generally located in tropical areas and separated from the ocean by coral reefs or atolls.

Crew I.D. card which doubles as a passport while in port.

LAKES

Smaller than seas, lakes are usually composed of fresh water and are almost always enclosed by land.

LAND ARRANGEMENTS

All services provided for the traveller by his tour operator after the traveller reaches his first foreign destination. Does not apply to overseas travel. Also referred to as ground arrangements.

LANDING GEAR

The undercarriage of an airplane, which consists of the wheels (or floats) upon which it moves when on the ground (or in the water).

The landing gear also supports the weight of the plane on the ground or in the water.

LANDING

When an aircraft touches down on the runway after a flight or returns to the ground.

LANDSIDE

The part of an airport that is publicly accessible (i.e., accessible to everyone who comes to the airport).

LATITUDE

Angular distance measured in degree north or south of the equator. One degree approximates 60 nautical miles.

LAYOVER

To a passenger this term refers to the time between flights at an airport. To an airline cabin crew this term refers to the time they are off duty at a city other than their domicile. In regards to crew, a layover period is the amount of time that separates two on-duty periods within a pattern or assignment. The layover station or city refers to the actual location of where you are off-duty for their rest period. For example, if a cabin crew arrives in Paris at 1800 and departs the next day at 2100, the layover period is 27 hours and the layover station is Paris.

LEAKAGES

Money that leave the local economy because it is used for taxation or the purchase of goods and services from outside the region. Leakages are used in calculations of the tourism income multiplier effect.

In tourism the term is used to signify the expenditure incurred on importation of goods and services for the use of the tourists or when money is put into savings and not re-invested.

LEARNING

Changes in a person's behaviour arising from experience.

LEEWARD

In the direction of the ship opposite from which the wind blows.

LEGACY CURRENCY

Refers to the former national currency of an EMU country, e.g. Deutsche Mark for Germany. After the introduction of EURO, Legacy Currency is no more in circulation in the countries where EURO is the legal tender.

LEISURE MARKET

Passengers who travel for recreational, or personal reasons.

LEISURE TOURISM

Tourism or travel for pleasure and relaxation as opposed to business. It can take place at home (domestic) or abroad (international) and for a variety of reasons.

LIFESTYLE

A person's pattern of living as expressed in his or her activities, interests, and opinions.

LIFT

The mechanical force that pushes a plane upward, against the gravitational pull. The movement of a plane's wing through the air creates lift.

LINE PERSONNEL

Personnel who interact directly with the customer.

LINE OF OPERATIONS SAFETY AUDIT (LOSA)

An audit practice that identifies precursors to accidents by looking closely at the threat and error side of crew performance, including how things such as bad weather and equipment malfunctions are handled and how mistakes are managed. Recently the International Civil Aviation Organization named LOSA a recommended practice for airlines around the world.

LINERS

Regular scheduled voyages on a set route on the sea or called 'Line voyages' and vessels (passenger or cargo) trading on these routes to a timetable are called liners. In older usages ' liner' also referred to ships of the line, i.e., line of-battle ship. This usage is now rare. Today, the term refers to a ship that is constructed to higher standard than a normal cruise ship, enabling it cross oceans such as Atlantic and Pacific with passengers, in inclement weather conditions.

LIQUOR CART

Also known as Liquor Kit or Wine Cart is a cart or compartment that contains liquor and wine that will be used during the flight for service. Depending on the class of service in which it is being used, the contents may be complimentary to the passenger or the Cabin Crew may be required charge for the selection made by the passenger.

LOAD FACTOR

The percentage of the total of an aircraft's capacity which has been sold.

LOAD FACTOR

Total Revenue Passenger kilometres divided by total aircraft seat kilometres (ASKs).

LOADING BRIDGE

A covered passageway from the airport terminal building to an aircraft for the use of the embarking and disembarking passengers.

LOBBYING

Dealing with legislator and government officials to promote or defeat legislation and regulation.In travel and tourism field, lobbying refers to helping the company achieve objectives by engaging influential contacts.

LOCAL COMBINATION

Combination of two fare components between the same points to create a single pricing unit.

LOCAL CURRENCY FARES

Fares and related charges expressed in the currency of the country of commencement of travel.

LOCATION, APPROVED

Sometimes referred to as 'Location', includes Head Office, Branch Office and Satellite Ticket Printer Locations appearing on the Agency List.

LODGE, TOURIST

A small house providing temporary accommodation to a tourist. The accommodation provided is inexpensive as compared to a conventional hotel. The lodge may also offers meals.

LONG HAUL TRAVEL

Long haul travel/flights are journeys typically made by the wide-body aircrafts like Boeing 747, Airbus A-380, Boeing 777 etc. that involve long distances, typically beyond seven hours in length and often are non-stop flights. On some long haul–flights for example from Delhi to New York or from Singapore to Los Angeles, Jet airlines may refuel in order to reach the destination.

LONGITUDE

Angular distance measured in degree east or west of the prime meridian of Greenwich, England (UTC).

LOST DOCUMENT

An Accountable Traffic Document which is no longer in the possession of its lawful custodian without having been identified as stolen.

LOW COST CARRIER (L C C)

A low cost carrier or a low cost airline (also known as a no –frill, discount or budget carrier or airline)is a airline that generally has lower fares.To make up for the revenue loss in decreased ticket sales, the airline may charge for extras like food, priority boarding, seat allocating, and baggage etc.The term originated within the airline industry referring to airline with a lower operating cost structure than their competitors.While the term is often applied with any carrier with low ticket prices and limited services, regardless of their operating models, low cost carriers are not to be confused with regional airlines that operate short flights without service, or with full service airlines offering some reduced fares.

LOW/OFF SEASON

Time of year when tourist traffic and rates are usually the lowest because demand is the lowest.

LOWER BED

A single bed placed at the conventional height from the floor.

LUXURY LINER

Also known as Cruise ship offers up market high level of comfort to the passengers. Primarily designed for affluent passengers, it is a resort on the floating water.

MACRO DESTINATIONS

Destinations that contain thousands of micro destinations, including regions, states, cities, towns, and even visitor destinations within a town.

MACRO-ENVIRONMENT

The larger societal forces that affect the whole micro environment: competitive, demographic, economic, natural, technological, political, and cultural forces.

MAIL, DIRECT

A form of promotion that involves the mailing of letters, flyers, postcards, brochures, questionnaires, newsletters or other printed materials to past, present and prospective clients.

MAJOR AIRLINES

Those large airlines that connect the major cities of the world. These airlines have the capability to handle international destinations and can fly just about anywhere in the world.

MANAGEMENT INFORMATION SYSTEM (MIS)

A "MIS "is a planned system of collecting, processing, storing and disseminating data in the form of information needed to carry out the functions of management. In a way, it is a documented report of the activities those were planned and executed.

A management information system is a subject of the overall internal control of a business covering the application of people, documents, technologies and procedures by management accountants to solve business problems such as costing a product, services or a business-wise strategy. Management information systems are distinct from regular information systems in that they are used to analyse other information systems applied in operational activities in the organization.

MANAGEMENT, CAPACITY

Managing the number of seats in an aircraft owned or operated by an airline.

MANAGEMENT, MARKETING

The analysis, planning, implementation, and control of programmes designed to create, built and maintain beneficial exchanges with target buyers for the purpose of achieving organizational objectives.

MANAGEMENT, REVENUE

Maximisation of profits from every flight and route network. Involves asking the questions like-how to determine, how many seats should be reserved for each fare type in order to maximize revenue from each flight.

MANIFEST

A list or invoice of a ship's passengers, crew and cargo.

MANUAL (INFLIGHT HANDBOOK, INFLIGHT MANUAL)

A handbook issued by the airline to the cabin crew. It contains all the regulations and procedures that are to be followed. It covers topics from emergencies, medical situations and service. The airlines and regulatory agencies require Cabin Crew to carry certain information contained in the manual with them at all times while on duty so that they have a reference. Cabin Crew will also be required to insert revised pages outlining new or changed procedures as required by the airline.

MARK UP

The extra amount added to the per person cost of a tour to get the final cost and is one of the main source of income for the travel agents and tour operators.

MARKET POSITIONING

Formulating competitive positioning for a product or a service and detailed marketing mix.

MARKET TARGETING

Evaluating each market segments' attractiveness and selecting one or more segments to enter.

MARKET INTERMEDIARIES

Firms that help the company to promote, sell and distribute its good to final buyers which include middlemen, physical distribution firms, marketing service agencies and financial intermediaries.

MARKET POTENTIAL

The total estimated dollars or unit value of a defined market for a defined product, including competitive products.

MARKET SEGMENTATION

The analysis, planning, implementation and control of programmes designed to create, build and maintain beneficial exchanges with target buyers for the purpose of achieving organizational objectives.

MARKET SEGMENTS

May also be known as price tiers. This distinguishes to the type of customer market targeted by the hotel. For example; luxury, corporate or budget.

MARKET TRENDS

External trends of many types that are likely to affect the marketing in which a corporation operates.

MARKET

The set of actual and potential buyers of product.

MARKET, AVAILABLE

The set of consumers that has interest, income, and access to a particular product.

MARKET, LEISURE

Passengers who travel for recreational, or personal reasons.

MARKET, POTENTIAL

The set of consumers who have professed some level of interest in a particular product.

MARKET, SERVED

Those consumers who have interest, income, access, and qualifications for the product or service.

MARKET-ORIENTED STRATEGIC PLANNING

The managerial process of developing and maintaining a viable fit between the organization's objectives, skills, and resources and its changing market opportunities.

MARKETING

A social and managerial process by which people and groups obtain what they need and want through creating and exchanging products and value with others.

A total activity which include an evaluation of market and the requirements of individuals within that market, together with an evaluation of service, facility or visitor plant, separately or jointly, its cost or accessibility, and the total facilities to provide visitor satisfaction. It includes merchandising programme aimed at particular type of customer to convert him to a user or purchaser of a service.

MARKETING CONCEPT

The marketing management philosophy which holds that achieving organizational goals depends on determining the needs and wants of target markets and delivering desired satisfactions more effectively and efficiently than competitors.

MARKETING DATABASE

An organized set of data about individual customers or prospects that can be used to generate and qualified customer leads, sell products and services, and maintain customer relation.

MARKETING ENVIRONMENT

The actions and forces outside marketing that affect marketing management's ability to develop and maintain successful transactions with its target customers.

MARKETING INFORMATION SYSTEM (MIS)

A structure of people, equipment, and procedures to gather sort, analysis, evaluate, and distribute needed, timely, and accurate information to marketing decision makers.

MARKETING INTELLIGENCE

Everyday information about development in the marketing environment that helps manager to prepare and adjust marketing plans.

MARKETING INTERMEDIARIES

Firms that help the company to promote, sell, and distribute its goods to final buyers; they include middlemen, physical distribution firms, marketing-service agencies, and financial intermediaries.

MARKETING MANAGEMENT

The analysis, planning, implementation, and control of programmes designed to create, built and maintain beneficial exchanges with target buyers for the purpose of achieving organizational objectives.

MARKETING MANAGER

A person who is involved in marketing analysis, planning, implementation, and control activities.

MARKETING MIX

A mixture of elements which interact and complement each other to achieve the targeted results. It is the combination of marketing variables that the firm uses to pursue to sought level of sales in the target market.

MARKETING OBJECTIVES

Quantitative and time specific achievements as to what is expected of a marketing programme.

MARKETING OPPORTUNITIES

An area of need in which a company can perform profitably.

MARKETING POSITIONING

Formulating competitive positioning for a product and detailed marketing mix.

MARKETING RESEARCH

The systematic design, collection, analysis, and reporting of data and findings relevant to a specific marketing situation facing a company.

MARKETING SHOPPING

An unobtrusive method of gathering data that uses people posing as bona fide shoppers to observe and collect information about an organization's service performance.

MARKETING STRATEGY DEVELOPMENT

Designing an initial marketing strategy for a new product based on the product concept.

MARKETING STRATEGY

The process of adjusting controllable marketing factors to cope with or exploit uncontrollable environment forces.

MARKETING TARGETING

Evaluating each market segments attractiveness and selecting one or more segments to enter.

MARKETING THREATS

A challenge posed by unfavourable trends or developments that would lead, in the absence of defensive marketing action, to sale or profit deterioration.

MARKETING, CONCENTRATED

A market-coverage strategy in which a firm goes after a large share of one or few submarkets.

MARKETING, DIFFERENTIATED

A market-coverage strategy in which a firm decides to target several market segments and designs separate offers for each.

MARKETING, DIRECT

Marketing through various advertising media that interact directly with consumers, generally calling for the consumers to make a direct response.

MARKETING, DIRECT-MAIL

Direct marketing through single mailing that include letters, ads, samples, foldouts, and other "salespeople on wings" sent to prospects on mailing lists.

MARKETING, INTERACTIVE

Marketing by a service firm to train effectively and motivate its customer-contact employees and depends heavily on the quality of buyer-seller interaction

MARKETING, MULTICHANNEL

Multichannel distribution, as when a single firm sets up two or more marketing channels to reach one or more customer segments.

MARKETING, RELATIONSHIP

Relationship marketing involves creating, maintaining and enhancing strong relationships with customers and other stakeholders.

MASS TOURISM

Mass tourism is the act of visiting a destination by a large number of people (tourists) at one time, and the study of effect that large number of people can have on a particular destination which has been over–exposed by single tourists or small number of tourists having been there repeatedly.

MASTER PLAN

A document that describes in narrative and with maps an overall development concept. The Master Plan is used to co-ordinate the preparation of more detailed plans or may be a collection of detailed plans. Master plan is prepared for the overall utilization of a particular area, including its allocation for residential or manufacturing uses and the corresponding environmental impacts.

MATURITY STAGE

The stage in a product life cycle when sales growth slows or levels off.

MAXIMUM PERMITTED MILEAGE

This refers to the full fare paying passengers right not to proceed directly from his place of origin to his destination but to stop over and vary his route by 20 percent of the minimum mileage without any surcharge.

MEAL PLANS

Inclusive packages offered by hotels for meals plus sleeping rooms.

MEASURABILITY

The degree to which the size and purchasing power of a market segment can be measured.

MEDIA IMPACT

The qualitative value of an exposure through a given medium.

MEDIA

Non-personal communication channels, including print media (newspapers, magazines, direct mail), broadcast media (radio, television), and display media (billboards, signs, posters).

MEDIA VEHICLES

Specific media within each general media type, such as specific magazines, television shows, or radio programmes.

MEDICAL TOURISM

Provision of cost effective private medical care in collaboration with the tourism industry for patients needing surgical and other forms of specialized treatment at an affordable price. It covers a broad spectrum of medical services. It mixes leisure, fun and relaxation together with wellness and healthcare.

MEDIUM-HAUL TRAVEL

Air travel of between four and six hour's duration is considered medium haul.

MEETING, CORPORATE

A meeting held by a corporation for its employees.

MEMBER, CREW

A qualified individual assigned by an air carrier to perform specific duties in an aircraft. Can also refer to pilots or cabin crew.

MESS

Mess is an area in the ship where food and drinks are served to the members which are part of the ship's crew.

Officers and crew have a dining room and kitchen separate from the passenger dining room and kitchen. Crew mess is generally open from about 6:30 am to 11:00 pm to accommodate the schedules of every department.

METAL FATIGUE

Refers to the fact that metal parts that undergo many repeated strains eventually fail at a loading far below their original ultimate strength.

METHOD, AFFORDABLE

Setting the promotion budget at what management thinks the company can afford.

MICRO MARKETING

A form of target marketing in which companies tailor their marketing programmes to the needs and wants of narrowly defined geographic, demographic, psychographic, or benefit segments.

MIDDLEMEN

Distribution channels firms that help a company find customers or make sales to them.

MILITARY RATES

Rates offered to military personnel and either negotiated or offered to promote business in areas close to military bases.

MINI BAR

Small refrigerator placed in the hotel room containing chocolates, souvenirs, sweet and salted and beverages both alcoholic and non-alcoholic.

MINIMUM CONNECTING TIME (MCT)

The shortest time interval necessary for transferring from one flight to another.

MINIMUM

Room usually reserved for overflow or emergency situations and often with distinct drawbacks.

MISCELLANEOUS CHARGE ORDER (MCO)

A voucher exchange with any IATA airline for flights, excess baggage etc. Instead of issuing an executive with a first class ticket, a company issues him with an MCO for the equivalent value. He flies to his business appointment economy class and later uses the remaining value of his vouchers to pay his holiday flights. MCO is a document issued by a travel agent for collecting money for the services which are related to air travel but of a nature which cannot be covered by an air ticket.

Miscellaneous charge order is an all purpose voucher issued by an airline and drawn on any organization such as accommodation, food and beverage, sightseeing, transfers etc. Which is willing to accept it in pre-payment for services or charges rendered to a customer.

MISCONNECTION

Occurs when a passenger is unable to use reserved accommodation out of a connection point due to late arrival or cancellation of delivering flight.

MISSING DOCUMENT

Means an Accountable Traffic Document which may or may not be in the possession of its lawfully custodian and for which research is in progress, pending recovery or reclassification as Lost or Stolen.

MODIFIED AMERICAN PLAN (MAP)

Includes two full meals per day in the price of a hotel room. Also referred to as Half Board.

MODULES

Elective tour variations during certain segments of an escorted tour.

MONOPOLISTIC COMPETITION

A market in which many buyers and sellers trade over a range of prices rather than a single market price.

MONORAIL

Monorail, railway system that uses cars that run on a single rail. Typically the rail is run overhead and the cars are either suspended from it or run above it. Driving power is transmitted from the cars to the track by means of wheels that rotate horizontally, making contact with the rail between its upper and lower flanges. In the Maglev monorails currently under development, powerful magnets hold the car just off its track and propel it at high speed. One of the principal advantages of a monorail is the relative simplicity of its tracks in comparison with that of a standard railway. Monorails originated and still function as materials-handling systems, similar to travelling cranes, for use in large factories. Short urban transportation monorails have been built in Houston, Seattle, and Germany. A maglev line linking Shanghai's financial district with its new airport began commercial operation. There is also a proposal to built monorail system in Delhi and Mumbai.

MONUMENTS

A permanent structure, building, erections etc.made at a place to mark the memory of a historical event, action, place or person etc. The structure is venerated for its enduring historic significance or association with a notable past person or a event.

MOTEL

A place which provides wayside amenities for tourists travelling by road, by automobiles. It provides under one roof all usual facilities expected by the tourists including attached bath, cafeteria, play room for children.

MOTIVATION

A driving force within an individual that impels him / her to an action towards satisfaction of needs.

MOTIVATORS

Those factors that make people want to achieve a particular goal.

MOTIVE

A need that is sufficiently pressing to direct a person to seek satisfaction of that need.

MOTOR COACH TOUR

A tour that utilizes motor coaches or buses to move tourists from one destination to another and to visit sight seeing attractions along the way. This type of tour gives ample opportunity for observing country / city sights.

MOUNTAINEERING

A specialized sport, which requires absolute physical fitness and determination on the part of mountaineer. The sport offer some flexibility in terms of time budget and skills required.

MULTI MEDIA

Multiple forms of information contents (e.g. text, audio,

graphics, animation, video, interactivity) to inform or entertain the (user) audience.

MULTICHANNEL MARKETING

Multichannel distribution, as when a single firm sets up two or more marketing channels to reach one or more customer segments.

MULTIPLE PURPOSE DOCUMENT (MPD)

A form used for automated issuance of interline accountable traffic documents other than the ticket. It is a multi-copy carbonized form or a documents issued coupon-by-coupon for use by carriers and travel agents.

MULTIPLIER EFFECT

Tourist expenditures that are recycled through the local economy, being spent and re spent.

MURPHY

A bed that folds into the wall when not in use. These are especially good when using the room to entertain or conducting business.

MUSTER DRILL

International maritime law requires all crew members to be placed at passenger emergency stations. During an emergency, passengers are assigned a muster station or meeting place such as a lounge or theatre. Crew members assist and guide passengers to the muster station. In short, muster personnel act as crowd control in the event of an emergency. Hospitality and entertainment departments are responsible for coordinating this exercise.

SECTION 5: N, O, P & Q

National tourism board, passenger fare, niche tourism, journeys, outbound tourism, planning, passenger name record, pre-paid ticket advise, product development, public sector tourism, public relations, promotion, leisure travel, pata, tourism product and miscellaneous.

NARROW-BODY JETS

A common class of traditional airlines which has a diameter of 3 to 4 metres (10 to 13 ft), a single aisle, and seats arranged 2 to 6 abreast. The largest narrow-body aircraft carry about 280 passengers.

NATIONAL PARK

An area, which is strictly reserved for wildlife and where activities such as forestry, grazing and cultivation are not permitted.

NATIONAL TOURISM OFFICE (NTO)

A national government or quasi government agency that markets destination tourism.

NATIONAL TOURIST BOARD

A government body set up to represent the tourism interests of a country. One of the key national tourist board's function is to promote its country abroad to attract foreign tourists.

NATIONAL TOURIST ORGANIZATION

The body responsible for the formulation and implementation of national tourist policy. It is the agency and instrument for the execution of the national governments responsibilities for the control, direction and promotion of tourism.

NATURAL ATTRACTIONS

These are well-defined natural features of a region. Visitors are generally drawn towards beautiful scenery, high mountains, forests, rivers, lakes coastlines and similar outstanding features.

NATURAL ENVIRONMENT

Natural resources that are needed as inputs by marketers or are affected by marketing activities.

NEGOTIATION

Verbal interaction between a client and a salesperson relative to the selling process.

NET RATE

A Wholesale Rate offered by the travel company to it's major bulk buyers. It is considerably lower than the rate which is offered to individual clients.

NETWORKING

To bring together different sectors working in the tourism industry to support new projects and initiatives such as guidelines for sustainable development.

NEUTRAL TICKET

The form of ticket for use by Travel Agents not bearing any preprinted individual airline identity.

NEUTRAL UNIT OF CONSTRUCTION (NUC)

Unit of common international value, such as a currency, established by IATA to calculate international air fares and charges.

NEW PRODUCT DEVELOPMENT

The development of original products, product improvements, product modifications, and new brands through a firm's own R & D efforts.

NEW PRODUCT

A good service, or idea that is perceived by some potential customers as new.

NEW RECEIVING CARRIER

Means a new carrying airlines selected for onward carriage by the forwarding carrier from the point where involuntary change of routing becomes necessary.

NICHE TOURISM

Tourism that combines elements designed to appeal those with certain narrow or special interest.

NICHE TOURISM

A small specialized sector which appeals to a correspondingly tightly defined market segment. Examples of the more common niche tourism markets include eco–tourism, agri-tourism, culinary tourism, heritage tourism, medical tourism, nautical tourism, space tourism, religious tourism, war tourism.

NO SHOW

The status of reservation when the guest does not arrive by the check in deadline. Also a passenger holding a flight reservation who fails to use it and cancel it prior to the flight departure.

NON REVENUE PASSENGER

A person travelling on a free or service charge only ticket. Airline employees travelling as part of their benefits are referred to as non-revenue/free pass riders.

NON-SCHEDULED FLIGHTS

Typically charter flights for travellers who want to hire a plane to fly to a specific place at a specific time.

NONPERSONAL COMMUNICATION CHANNEL

Media that carry messages without personal contact or feedback, including media atmosphere and events.

NORMAL FARE

A fare established for intermediate, first or economy class service and any other fare denominated and published as a normal fare (e.g. C2, F2, Y2). Children's fares and infant's fares which are established as a percentage of the fares referred to above are also considered to be normal fares.

NORMS

Describes how things get done in an organization.

NORTH ATLANTIC TREATY ORGANIZATION (NATO)

NATO was formed in 1949 as a defensive alliance by the US, Canada, and Many European countries worried about the threat of the Soviet Union. In this alliance, the member nations pledged that an attack against one would be considered an attack against all. During the Cold War, NATO was the main military coordinating body of the nations that opposed the spread of communism. Even with the collapse of communism in Russia and its satellite countries, NATO remains an important force in world affairs including travel and tourism.

OBJECTION

A concern, worry, question, or other barrier to a potential client making a commitment to buy something that they need or want.

OBJECTIVE AND TASK METHOD

Developing the promotion budget by (1) defining specific objectives, (2) determining the tasks that must be performed to achieve these objectives, and (3) estimating the costs of performing these tasks; the sum of these costs is the proposed promotion budget.

OBJECTIVE, ADVERTISING

A specific communication task to be accomplished with a specific target audience during a specific period of time.

OBJECTIVES, MARKETING

Quantitative and time specific achievements as to what is expected of a marketing programme.

OBSERVATIONAL RESEARCH

The gathering of primary data by observing relevant people, actions, and situations.

OCCUPANCY, SINGLE

Sole occupancy of a cabin that is designed to accommodate two or more passengers, in which instance a premium is ordinarily charged.

OCCUPANCY

Room occupancy from the agents perspective is the rate charged per person. It may be charged as a single or double (e.g. single occupancy, double occupancy etc.). From the hotels perspective, occupancy means the number of guests the hotel is accommodating on any given night (e.g. 80% occupancy of a 400 room hotel would be 320 rooms sold).

OFF-PREMISE TRANSITIONAL AUTOMATED TICKET (OPTAT)

Either form of automated ticket, normally issued by agents which is a multi-copy carbonized ticket.

OFFER

The cruise line's commitment for accommodation when available which may be suited to the passenger's needs or wishes.

OFFICIAL AIRLINE GUIDE (OAG)

A publication containing all airline routes, schedules and airport information.

OMBUDSMAN

Official appointed to investigate individual's complaint against public authorities.

ON REQUEST

Refers to the status of a seat request. (i.e., not yet confirmed).

ONE WAY SUB JOURNEY

Part of a journey wherein travel from one country does not return to such country and for which the fare is assessed as a single pricing unit using a one way fare.

ONLINE TRANSFER

Transfer from the service of one carrier to another service of the same carrier.

OPEN SEATING

Free access to unoccupied tables in the ship's dining room, as opposed to specific table assignments.

OPEN SKIES

Refers to either to a bilateral (between two countries) or multilateral (involving more than two countries) Air Transport Agreement which liberalises the rules for international aviation markets and minimize government intervention.

OPEN SOURCE SOFTWARE

Software that is made available to the general public with either relaxed or non-existent intellectual property restrictions.

OPEN TICKET

A ticket which has been issued for a particular journey but on which a specific date has yet to be entered.

OPEN-END QUESTIONS

Questions that allow respondents to answer in their own words.

OPERATING SYSTEM SOFTWARE

Operating system software is the software that creates the environment in which your personal computer can work. For example, it interprets your keyboard, mouse, etc. it controls your printers, stores and retrieves information and displays the information on your monitor.

OPERATIONS, AIRPORT

The ground facilities for air travel, including runways and navigation aids.

OPERATOR, TOUR

A person or business entity that is responsible for the actual implementation and operation of the tour with the tour participants. A travel organization that puts together inclusive tours. It buys the components (travel, accommodation, transfers) from principals and sells the complete package for an all inclusive price. A tour operator may use travel agents or sell direct to tourists.

OPINION LEADERS

People within a reference group who, because of special skills, knowledge, personality, of other characteristics, exert influence on others.

OPTIONAL

In travel literature the word means that the traveller has a choice of taking or not taking the service mentioned. If he takes it, there is always an additional charge which is not included in the basic tour price.

OPTION

The cruise line's offering of a specific cabin (or guarantee) for a specified period of time during which the passenger decides whether or not to accept. Acceptance is confirmed either by deposit or final payment.

ORDER, EXCHANGE

A document issued by a carrier or its agents requesting issue of an appropriate ticket or provision of services to the person named in such document.

ORGANIZATIONAL CULTURE

Refers to the personally of a company; what the organization believes in, strives for, and actually practices.

ORGANIZATIONAL STRUCTURE

Refers to the relationships, roles and responsibilities, authority and accountability that exist in a company.

ORGANIZATION IMAGE

The way a person or group views an organization.

ORGANIZATIONAL BUYING

The decision-making process by which formal organizations establish the need for purchased products and services and identify, evaluate, and choose among alternative brands and suppliers.

ORGANIZATIONAL CULTURE

The pattern of shared values and beliefs that gives members of an organization meaning and provides them with the rules for behaviour in that organization.

ORIGINAL RECEIVING CARRIER

Means the carrier on whose flight a passenger is originally ticketed to be carried from a connection point.

ORIGIN

The initial starting place of the journey as shown on the ticket.

OTHER CHARGES

Charges such as taxes, fees, etc., excluding excess baggage charges.

OUTBOUND TOURISM

International tourism seen from the point of view of the originating country. Outbound tourism is a form of importation of services from abroad and as such has a negative effect on that country's tourism account.

OUTSIDE CABIN

A cabin having window(s) or porthole(s) offering a view of the sea or river.

OUTSOURCING

The contracting of services to external companies.

OUTSTANDING CABIN

A cabin having window (s) or porthole (s) offering a view of the sea or river.

OVERBOOKING

The practice of booking more rooms than the hotel's capacity of rooms by a hotel in anticipation of cancellations or no shows.In a similar manner an airlines may also overbook the seats than aircraft's capacity of seats in anticipation of cancellations or no shows.

OVERHEAD LOCKERS (OVERHEAD BINS)

Compartments installed above the seats in an aircraft that are used by passengers to place their belongings including carry-on luggage.

OVERRIDE

An additional commission paid by the supplier as a sales incentive to agents who provide more business.

OVERRIDING COMMISSION

An additional commission paid by a principal such as an airline or a tour operator, to a travel agent as a bonus or an incentive to generate high sales.

PA SYSTEM

Public address system used to make announcements in an aircraft or a tourist coach to give specific information to passengers concerning their travel.

PACIFIC ASIA TRAVEL ASSOCIATION (PATA)

Pacific Asia Travel Association was formed in the year 1951 as an non–profit corporation to stimulate interest in the Pacific region as a vacation land, and, to develop, promote and facilitate travel to and among many pacific destinations. With Headquarters in Bangkok, is an international organization with over 2500 members made up from the Destinations, Carriers, Hotel Groups, Tour Operators, Ground Handlers and Retail Travel Agents, mainly based in the Pacific Asia Region. Other 'International' members include publications, travel writers and any organization with interests in travel to and within the Region.The principle philosophy of PATA is that the entire travel industry must work together to develop an ever–increasing flow of holiday leisure travel from which member of the association derives the fair share of the total business.

PACKAGE RATES

Negotiated with wholesalers who book large volume business.

PACKAGE TRAVEL DIRECTIVES

A European Union Directive (the Package Travel, Package Tour and Package Holiday Regulations, 1991) designed to offer consumers of inclusive tours financial security and certain minimum standards. Requires all organizations arranging package tours to be licensed and bounded to guarantee repayment of clients money in the event of bankruptcy of the company.

PACKAGE

An inclusive set of products or services designed to attract the leisure traveller. It normally includes all the elements of travel like transport, accommodation, meals, sightseeing etc.

PACKAGING, DYNAMIC

Websites mimic the experience of visiting a travel agent and negotiate a deal the consumer wants. Websites also allow the travel agent to package their own holidays and make better margins, while still offering a competitive price.

PACKAGING

The practice of combining different elements of the products and services (often from different firms) into a single package for one price. Travel package for example often include airfare, hotel, meals, sight-seeing for a single price.

PADDLE WHEEL

A wheel with boards around its circumference and commonly the sole source of propulsion for riverboats.

PARA SAILING

Winching or towing a parachutist to a height of a few hundred feet in the air and then descending by means of a parachute.

PARACHUTING

Jumping off from an aircraft or balloon and descending by means of a parachute.

PARK, NATIONAL

An area, which is strictly reserved for wildlife and where activities such as forestry, grazing and cultivation are not permitted.

PARTICIPATING CARRIER

A carrier over whose routes one or more sections of carriage under the ticket is undertaken or performed.

PASS, BOARDING

Boarding pass or a boarding card indicates the name, class, flight number, seat number allocated to a passenger. This is normally issued at check-in counter in exchange for passenger ticket coupon.

PASSENGER LOAD FACTOR (PLF)

Measure of how well an airline is balancing the capacity it makes available with the traffic it is able to attract. It compares the actual passenger traffic to the capacity available on a given flight. In other words, the PLF is the percentage of seating capacity actually used by customers as calculated by relationship between the RPKs and ASKs flown.

PASSENGER (PAX)

Person travelling and is often referred to in shortened form as PAX.

PASSENGER COUPON OR RECEIPT

Portion of the passenger's ticket and baggage check issued by or on behalf of a carrier, which constitutes the passenger's written evidence of the contract of carriage.

PASSENGER LOAD

Total number of passengers on the aircraft.

PASSENGER NAME RECORD (PNR)

A record of each passenger's travel requirements which contain all information necessary to enable reservations to be processed and controlled by the booking airline and the airline(s) participating in the carriage.

A unique computerized file. A PNR is created by the booking agent and is used to communicate passenger details and intended flight itinerary as well as other requests and information relevant to the carrier. Also referred to as booking or reservation.

PASSENGER SEAT FACTOR (PSF)

The passenger seat factor is a percentage measure of seat occupancy on a flight. However, in itself, a high PSF does not mean that the airline is making money. The flights could be having high occupancy because of the low fare offered.

PASSENGER TRANSFER

A passenger arriving on the flight and continuing his journey on another.

PASSENGER TRANSIT

A passenger continuing his journey in the same through flight.

PASSENGER, NON REVENUE

A person travelling on a free or service charge only ticket. Airline employees travelling as part of their benefits are referred to as non-revenue or pass riders.

PASSENGER, THROUGH

A person continuing on a flight through an intermediate stop to a further destination.

PASSENGER, TRANSIT

A person continuing on a flight through an intermediate (transit) stop, and is also referred to as a "through-passenger".

PASSENGER

Any person, except members of the crew, carried or to be carried in an aircraft with the consent of the carrier.

PASSENGER SERVICE UNIT OR PSU

Located above the passenger seats, it contains all or part of the following : Reading lights, air outlets, oxygen outlet, cabin crew call button, emergency oxygen mask and No Smoking and Fasten Seat Belt signs.

PASSPORT

A formal document issued by a government that identifies the holder as a national or citizen of that country. This document allows the holder to enter and pass through other countries at the request of the issuing country. It allows for legal protection abroad and the right to enter the person's country of nationality. It contains the holder's photograph, signature, date of birth and nationality. Over time, the League of Nations, United Nations and ICAO have issued guidelines of standardization for the layouts and the features of passports. These are seen in the passports of today.

PATH, FLIGHT

The direction of an aircraft in the air.

PATRONAGE REWARDS

Cash or other awards for the regular use of a certain company's products or services.

PATTERN, CREW

A term that refers to a schedule of assignments in sequence of one or more duty periods (working days) that begin and end in one's domicile.

PENSION

A French word widely used throughout Europe, meaning guesthouse or boarding house.The establishments are used extensively by the tourists. Catering facilities in these establishments are usually restricted to the residents.Many clients stay for a longer and definite periods such as a week, fortnight or even a month.In most cases the reservation is made in advance.

PENTHOUSE SUITE

The suite in the hotel which is located on the top floor of the hotel building giving a panoramic view.

PER DIEM

The cost for one day.

PERCENTAGE-OF-SALES METHOD

Setting the promotion budget at a certain percentage of current or forecasted sales or as a percentage of the sales price.

PERCEPTION

The process by which a person selects, organizes, and interprets information inputs to create a meaningful picture of the world.

PERFORMANCE REVIEW

The stage of an industrial buying process in which a buyer rates its satisfaction with suppliers, deciding whether to continue, modify, or drop the relationship.

PERISHABILITY

A fundamental characteristic of services referring to the fact that most services cannot be produced and stored before consumption; they exist only at the time of their production.

PERISHABLE PRODUCT

A product which has a particular life span after which it does not have any value.A airline seat not sold on a particular flight can not be stored and used in the next flight.

PERSONAL COMMUNICATION CHANNELS

Channels through which two or more people communicate directly with each other, including face to face, person to audience, over the telephone, or through the mail.

PERSONAL DIGITAL ASSISTANT

A lightweight and mobile electronic device that performs specific tasks such as a diary, calculator, contact database etc. One might use a PDA if one is working away from the office and needed to keep track of all appointments, contacts and daily information.

PERSONAL INFLUENCE

The effect of statements made by one person on another's attitude or probability of purchase.

PERSONAL SELLING

Oral presentation in a conversation with one or more prospective purchasers for the purpose of making sales.

PERSONNEL, LINE

Personnel who interacts directly with the customer.

PERSUASIVE ADVERTISING

Advertising used to build selective demand for a brand by persuading consumers it offers the best quality for their money.

PERSONALITY

A person's distinguishing psychological characteristics that lead to relatively consistent and lasting responses to his or her environment.

PHYSICAL DISTRIBUTION FIRMS

Warehouse, transportation, and other firms that help a company stock and move goods from their points of origin to their destinations.

PHYSICAL EVIDENCE

Tangible clues such as promotional material, employees of the firm and the physical environment of the firm. Physical evidence is used by a service firm to make its product more tangible to customers.

PHYSICAL

The spatial, finite capacity of a tourist resort or facility such as the land available. The total number of bed spaces and parking spaces.

PILOT

A certifies airman qualified to operate the controls of an aircraft in flight.

PITCH

The alternative rise and fall of a ship's bow which may occur when underway.

PITCH

The movement of the plane as its nose moves up or down.

PLAN, AMERICAN (AP)

A meal plan in hotel which includes all the three meals a day. Also referred to as "full board". American Plans are seldom used any more but may be offered in certain resorts or as part of package.

PLAN, CONTINENTAL

Daily hotel rate which includes accommodation and breakfast.

PLAN, DECK

An overhead diagram illustrating cabin and public room locations in relation to each other.

PLAN, EUROPEAN

Hotel accommodation with no meals whatsoever included in the cost of the tariff of the room.

PLAN, FLIGHT

Detailed document completed by the captain prior to every flight. It includes the planned routing, flying time, altitude and amount of fuel on board and an alternate airport if the plane is unable to land at the original destination airport.

PLANNING (DESTINATION LEVEL)

The organization and development of visitor attractions and services in and around destination communities.

PLANNING (SITE LEVEL)

Site Level planning involves the planning, design and development of individual tourist attractions, services and facilities to serve tourist needs.

PLANNING, STRATEGIC CORPORATE

Long-run planning that incorporates defining the mission statement, establishing strategic business units, assigning resources to each SBU, planning new business.

PLATEAU

A broad, flat area that rises above the surrounding landscape and because of its elevation, experiences a cooler climate on top.

POINT OF PURCHASE PROMOTION

Displays and demonstrations that take place at point of purchase or sale.

POINT OF TURNAROUND

The farthest geographical fare break point (between two fare components) from the Pricing Unit origin.

POINT – TO – POINT

Favoured by the trans-Atlantic carriers and those on the Hongkong / London and Australia routes. It offers a discount on the full fare return for the passenger sacrificing rights or stopover and utilize the maximum permitted mileage.

POINT, ASSEMBLY

A point in the itinerary where the entire qualifying group assembles and commences transportation as a group.

POINT-OF-PURCHASE PROMOTIONS (POP)

Displays and demonstrations that take place at the point of purchase or sale.

POLICY, TOURISM

Guidelines and decisions designed to assist the tourism industry in meeting objectives and goals. Tourism policy usually result from the actions of the governments various agencies and organizations.

POLITICAL ENVIRONMENT

Laws, government agencies, and pressure groups that influence and limit various organizations and individuals in a given society.

POLLUTION

Any noticeable change to the atmosphere beyond natural occurrences. It is introduction of containments into an environment of whatever predetermined or agreed upon proportions. These contaminants cause instability, disorder, harm or discomfort to the physical system or living organisms therein.

PORT

A term used to refer to the left hand side of the aircraft. (Also referred to as aircraft left).

PORTFOLIO, CUSTOMER

A term used to denote the mix of customers a particular service organization may target to ensure that all customer segments are desirable and compatible with one another.

PORT

The left side of the ship when facing towards the bow.

POSITIONING SYSTEM, GLOBAL (GPS)

The use of satellites to convey the positions of airplanes to air traffic controllers.

POSITIONING, MARKETING

Formulating competitive positioning for a product and detailed marketing mix.

POSITIONING

An organization's effort to establish consumer perceptions of a product in relation to all other products and substitutes.

POSTER

A pictorial representation of an idea. It is intended to attract attention rapidly to a single word or an idea.

POSTPURCHASE BEHAVIOUR

The stage of the buyer decision process in which consumers take further action after the purchase based on their satisfaction or dissatisfaction.

POTENTIAL MARKET

The set of consumers who have professed some level of interest in a particular product.

POTENTIAL TOURIST

A person who is likely to purchase a tourism product or can become a tourist at a later date. He may be withholding the purchase in the present time because of certain personal reasons and not because he cannot afford to buy.

POTHOLING

Potholing also called caving, is essentially about exploring caves.

PREMIUMS

Goods offered either free or at low cost as an incentive to buy a product.

PREPAID TICKET ADVISE (PTA)

Prepaid ticket advise or PTA is the notification by a computer message or commercial telex or mail that a person in one city (sponsor) has requested the issuance of transportation documents and has prepaid for the same on behalf of another person (passenger) in another city. The use of PTA permits the issuance of a ticket at a city other than that of a city where the payment is made.

PTA is the name given to the document asking a carrier to issue a ticket in favour of a person beginning his journey in a place other than that where payment was made.

PRESS RELATIONS

The aim of press relations is to place noteworthy information into the news media to attract attention to a person, product or service.

PRESSURISATION

The process of pumping air into the fuselage to maintain the atmospheric conditions inside the aircraft the same as those on the ground. Pressurization occurs at 2400 meters.

PRICE ELASTICITY

A measure of the sensitivity of demand to changes in price.

PRICE

The cost of a product or service.

PRICING UNIT

A journey or part of a journey which is priced as a separate entity, i.e. is capable of being ticketed separately.

PRIMARY DATA COLLECTION (TOURISM DATA)

Primary research or field research is original data generated by research carried out in tourist generating market. It involves first hand data (information) collection. Primary research covers both quantitative and qualitative data. The data collection techniques include interviews, sample surveys and observations.

PRIMARY DATA

Information collected for specific purpose at hand.

PRINCIPAL

Prime provider of travel and tourism services e.g. a carrier, an accommodation and ancillary services provider for whom travel agents act and from whom clients may also buy direct.

PRINT ADVERTISING

A form of marketing that uses print media such as newspapers, periodicals, guide books, and telephone directories to reach its target audience.

PRIVATE SECTOR TOURISM

That sector of the tourism industry, which is planned, financed and operated by the privately owned organization. Most of the tourism business in the world such as hotels, car hire companies, amusement parks, entertainment centres, transport organizations, tourist attractions, travel agencies and tour operators are owned and operated by private sector.

PROBLEM RECOGNITION

The stage of the industrial buying process in which someone in a company recognizes a problem or need that can be met by acquiring a good or a service.

PROCEDURE, APPLICANT RATING

A procedure used by companies to rank prospective members of the sales force.

PROCESS, ADOPTION

The mental process through which a person passes from first hearing about an innovation to final adoption.

PRODUCT CONCEPT

The idea that consumers will favour products that offer the most quality, performance and features and therefore the organization should devote its energy to making continuous product improvements.

PRODUCT DESIGN

The process of designing a product's style and function: creating a product that is attractive; easy, safe, and inexpensive to use and service; and simple and economical to produce and distribute.

PRODUCT DEVELOPMENT

Developing the product concept into a physical product concept to assure that the product idea can turned into a workable product.

PRODUCT FEATURES

Product features that enhance customer satisfaction is one type of service quality.

PRODUCT IDEA

An idea for a possible product that a company can anticipate offering to the market.

PRODUCT IMAGE

The way consumers picture an actual or potential product.

PRODUCT LIFE – CYCLE (PLC)

The course of a products sales and profits over its lifetime. It involves five distinct stages: product development, introduction, growth, maturity and decline.

PRODUCT LINE

A group of products that are closely related either because they function in a similar manner, are sold to the same customer groups, are marketed through the same types of outlets, or fall within given price ranges.

PRODUCT MIX (or product assortment)

The set of all product lines and items that a particular seller offers for sale to buyers.

PRODUCT POSITION

The way a product is defined by consumers on important attributes, the place, the product occupies in consumers minds relative to competing products.

PRODUCT PUBLICITY

Various efforts to publicize specific products.

PRODUCT SPECIFICATION

The stage of an industrial buying process in which the buying organization decides on and specifies the best technical product characteristics for a needed item.

PRODUCT, AUGMENTED

Additional consumer services and benefits built around the core and actual products.

PRODUCT, ACTUAL

A Product's parts, styling features, brand name, packaging, and other attributes that combine to deliver core product benefits.

PRODUCT, CORE

The central feature or benefit sought by the customer and offered by the service providers as a solution to customers needs and wants.

PRODUCT, INTANGIBLE

A service that cannot be touched.

PRODUCT-STRUCTURED SALES FORCE

A sales force structured along product lines.

PRODUCT

Anything that can be offered to a market for attention, acquisition, use or consumption that might satisfy a want or need. It includes physical objects, services, persons, places, organizations and ideas.

PROGRAMME, AIRPORT SECURITY

In order to protect civil aviation, each airport is

required by their national government to establish and implement an Airport Security Programme, which is primarily directed towards the prevention of and response to unlawful interference and threats to passengers, cargo and aircraft.

PROMOTION

All activities in producing and increasing sales including advertising, publicity, personal selling. The activities that supplement and make more effective advertising and personal selling. Special events individually treated to bring public attention to special products.

PROMOTION MIX

The specific mix of advertising, personal selling, sales promotion and public relations a company uses to pursue its advertising and marketing objectives.

PROMOTION, CONSUMER

Sales promotions designed to stimulate consumer purchasing, including samples, coupons, rebates, prices-off, premiums, patronage rewards, displays, and sweepstakes.

PROMOTION, SALES

Short term incentives to encourage purchase or sales of a product or service.

PROMOTIONAL RATES

Reduced rate generally offered when the hotel is not full to generate extra revenue.

PROPERTY

Another term for hotel or accommodation facility.

PROSPECT

A potential customer.

PROSPECTING

Research and activity in pursuit of potential clients for company's product or service that the company is selling.

PSYCHO-CENTRIC TRAVELLER

Seeks familiar, tried and tested destinations which are secure and is an unadventurous traveller.

PSYCHOCENTRIC

A description of a type of a tourist. Psychocentrics are those who are generally insecure, anxious and not at all self-confident people. They often return to familiar and known holiday resorts each year, where they feel safe and secure. They would require services of a guide or escort and would probably choose coach tours or stay in their own country of residence.

PSYCHOGRAPHIC SEGMENTATION

Dividing the market into different groups based on social class, lifestyle, or personality characteristics.

PSYCHOGRAPHIC

The technique of measuring and developing lifestyles classifications, involves measuring the major dimensions (activities, interests and opinions).

PUBLIC RELATION

Building good relations with a company's various publics by way of obtaining favourable publicity, building up a good corporate image and handling unfavourable rumours, stories and events. Major public relation tools include press relations, product publicity, corporate communications, lobbying and counselling.

PUBLIC SECTOR TOURISM

Tourism organizations and enterprises funded by government and generally for the benefit of society as a whole are known as a tourist information office or a national tourist board. Majority of the National Tourism Organizations such as airlines, rail systems, airports, may also be publicly owned and managed. The provision of service to the general public is the main consideration rather than profit motive.

PUBLIC

Any group that has an actual or potential interest in or impact on an organization's ability to achieve its objectives.

PUBLICITY

Activities to promote a company or its products by planting news about it in media not paid for by the sponsor.

PULL STRATEGY

A promotion strategy that calls for spending a lot on advertising and consumer promotion to build up consumer demand; if successful, consumers will ask the wholesalers, and the wholesalers in turn will ask the producers.

PURCHASE DECISION

The stage of the buyer's decision process in which the consumer actually buys the product.

PURE COMPETITION

A market in which many buyers and sellers trade in a uniform commodity; no single buyer or seller has much effect on the going market price.

PURSER

The person who is in charge of the cabin crew. Some airlines refer to this position as Lead or Senior Flight

Attendant. The purser is responsible for coordinating the crew and their duties, completion of paperwork and international customs documents. Often this position requires additional training or qualification by an airline including service, conflict resolution and company procedures and other management skills.

PUSH PROMOTIONAL STRATEGY

A process of maximizing the use of all available channels of distribution to " push "the product or service into the market place. This usually requires generous discounts to achieve the objective of giving the channels incentive to promote the product or service, thus minimizing the need for advertising.

PUSH STRATEGY

A promotion strategy that calls for using the sales force and trade promotion to push the product through channels; the producer promotes the product to wholesalers, the wholesalers promote to retailers, and the retailers promote to consumers.

PORT AND STARBOARD

The original fishing boats in the south of England were equipped with a "steer board" that hung over the side (unlike a tiller, which hangs over the stern). This solved the problem of nets getting caught in the steering apparatus when set off the stern of the vessel. Most fishermen were right handed, consequently placing the steer board over the right side. To save the steer board apparatus from damage while in port, the left side of the boat was tied to the dock, leaving the steer board away from the dock. To this day we refer to the right as starboard (from steer board) and left as port. A good way to keep them straight: "left" has the same number of letters as "port," which is the left side of the boat when facing forward.

QUALIFYING

The process of determining the sales potential and probability of obtaining and closing an account.

QUALITY

The totality of features and characteristics of a product that bear on its ability to meet customer need.

QUARANTINE

When humans or animals are kept away from others to reduce the spread of communicable disease.

QUEEN

An extra large double bed smaller than the king.

QUESTIONS, CLOSED-END

Questions that include all the possible answers and allow subjects to make choices among them.

QUOTES

Quantitative and time-specific accomplishment measurements established for members of a sales force.

SECTION 6: R & S

Travel retailing, rural tourism, resorts, tourism research, responsible tourism, round trip, airline reservations, routes, seasonality, tourism planning and environment, customer satisfaction, accommodation, social tourism, schengen, visa, sustainability, special interest tourism, safety in aircraft and miscellaneous.

RACK RATE

The official rate advertised by a hotel company or other tourism provider. This is the rate "across the counter", the one offered to the public before any discounts are applied.

RADIO FREQUENCY IDENTIFICATION (RFID)

A means of simplifying airline baggage management by eliminating manual encoding.

RAIL TOUR

A tour in which primary mode of transport during the tour is by train.

RAMP (APRON, TARMAC)

The paved area on the field side of the terminal building where aircraft are parked to load and unload passengers.

RAPPORT

Building a level of understanding and trust with a prospect so that they will be willing to have you help them get their needs met.

RATE, CATEGORIES

Rate categories indicate the amount of money hotels charge for a room and the various discounts available within the initially quoted price.

RATE, CONSORTIUM

Negotiated rated based on volume.

RATE, CORPORATE

Rates typically offered to the business travellers ranging from 20 - 30% off rack rate.

RATE, DAY

Special rate for the use of a room during the day from approx 0800 hours to 1800 hours.

RATES, SEASONAL

Variations in prices for the same service, depending upon the time of the year.

RATIONAL APPEALS

Message appeals that relate to an audience's self-interest and show that the product will produce the claimed benefit; examples include appeals to product quality, economy, value, or performance.

RE-BOOKING

Change of reservation or other changes which do not require ticket reissuance.

REACH

The percentage of people in the target market exposed to an ad campaign during a given period.

RECEIVING CARRIER

The airline which transports the passenger after he arrives at an interline point.

RECESSION TOURISM

Recession tourism is a travel trend, which evolved by way of the world economic crisis. Recession tourism is defined by low-cost, high-value experiences taking place of once-popular generic retreats. Various recession tourism hotspots have seen business boom during the recession. Thanks to comparatively low costs of living and a slow world job market suggesting travellers are stretching out trips where the dollar travels further.

RECOMMENDED PRACTICE

A specification for physical characteristics or performance of a facility or personnel, the uniform application of which is recognized as desirable.

RECONFIRMATION

Procedure (normally a telephone call to the airline from which ticket has been purchased and confirmed) by which passengers confirm their intention to use the reserved seat booking.

RECORDER, FLIGHT DATA

A device that records aircraft performance parameters. It is an aid to study air safety issues, material and jet performance and is also used in aircraft accident analysis.

REDUNDANCY

The duplication of critical components of an aircraft system, which have been purposely "built-in" in order to increase reliability and safety.

REFERENCE GROUPS

Groups that have a direct (face-to-face) or indirect influence on a person's attitude or behaviour.

REFUND

The repayment to the purchaser of all or portion of a fare or change for unused carriage or service.

REGIONAL AIRLINES

Feeder airlines whose role is to bring passengers to the major hubs, where they will connect for longer distance flights on larger aircraft.

REGIONAL PLANNING

Is a branch of land use planning and deals with the efficient placement of land use activities, infrastructure, and settlement growth across a significantly larger area of land than an individual city or town. The related field of urban planning deals with the specific issues of city planning. Both concepts are encapsulated in spatial planning.

REGISTRY

The country under whose laws the ship and its owners are obliged to comply, in addition to compliance with the laws of the countries at which the ship calls and / or embarks or disembarks passengers / cargo.

RELATED CHARGES

Such as cancellation penalties, non-refundable amounts, rebooking and rerouting charges, stopover charges, weekend surcharges etc. & excess baggage charges.

RELATIONSHIP MARKETING

Relationship marketing involves creating, maintaining and enhancing strong relationships with customers and other stakeholders.

REMINDER ADVERTISING

Advertising used to keep consumers thinking about a product.

REPORT TIME (SHOW TIME)

The time the flight crew or cabin crew is required to report for duty at the airport.

REPOSITIONING CRUISE

When a cruise ship relocates from one cruise regions itinerary to a new cruise region itinerary, it makes a special sailing en route to the new area stopping in ports-of-call along the way.

REROUTING

With respect to a passenger, means a change of route, fare, carrier, type of aircraft, class of service, flight or validity from that originally provided in the appropriate transportation document.

RESEARCH, CASUAL

Marketing research to rest hypotheses about and-effect-relationships.

RESEARCH, CASUAL- COMPARATIVE

Also known as ex - post - facto research, this is research that attempts to determine the cause, or reason, for existing differences in the behaviour or status of groups of individuals. It usually involves starting with and effect and seeking possible causes.

RESEARCH, CORRELATIONAL

Attempts to determine whether, and to what degree, a relationship exists between two or more quantifiable variables. The purpose is to establish a relationship (or lack of it) or to use relationships in making predictions.

RESEARCH, DESCRIPTIVE

Marketing research to better describe marketing problems, situations, or markets, such as the market potential for a product or the demographics and attitudes of consumers. It involves collecting data in order to test hypotheses or answer questions concerning the current status of the subject of the study. Data are typically collected through a questionnaire survey, an interview, or observation.

RESEARCH, EXPERIMENTAL

The gathering of primary data by selecting matched groups of subjects, giving them different treatments, controlling related factors, and checking for differences in group responses. The researcher manipulates at least one independent variable (cause) and observes the effect on one or more dependent variables (effect).

RESEARCH, EXPLORATORY

Marketing research to gather preliminary information that will help to better define problems and suggest hypotheses.

RESEARCH, HISTORICAL

The studying, understanding, and explaining of past events. The purpose of historical research is to arrive at conclusions concerning causes, effects, or trends of past occurrences that may help explain present events and anticipate future events.

RESEARCH, MARKETING

The systematic design, collection, analysis, and reporting of data and findings relevant to a specific marketing situation facing a company.

RESEARCH, OBSERVATIONAL

The gathering of primary data by observing relevant people, actions, and situations.

RESERVATION

Equivalent to the term booking. The allotment in advance of seating or sleeping accommodation for a passenger or of a space or weight capacity for baggage.

RESERVATION, CONFIRMED

A definite booking where seats are available and a reservation has been created under a passengers name.

Oral or written statement by a supplier that the request for a reservation has been received and will be honored.

RESERVE

The status of cabin crew who is on-call for the entire month. He or she may be requested to work a trip when someone is sick, on vacation, or late for his or her or assigned flight.

RESORT AND RESORT COMPLEX

A self-contained site which provides all or most of the products and services required by a tourist. They tend to combine attractions with support services such as accommodation and catering.

RESORT HOTEL

In addition to the facilities provided in the city hotels, resort hotels provide attractions such as swimming pools, private beaches, sport facilities like tennis courts and other outdoor and indoor recreational facilities. Resort hotels are situated in areas of scenic beauty, sightseeing attractions or in the surroundings providing entertainment opportunities. These could be of various types like beach resorts, health resorts, winter resorts etc.

RESORT RATES

These rates can fluctuate based on advance payment, deposits, season or individual property agreements.

RESORT, BEACH

A self-contained site which provides all or most of the products and services required by guest (a tourist). These tend to combine attractions with support services such as accommodation and catering.

RESPONSIBLE TOURISM

A form of tourism that advocates smaller scale and limited tourism in term of numbers of tourists involved and the dimension of tourism development. It is also called green tourism or alternative tourism.

REST AND RECREATION

Specified time usually included in most planned tours to allow the traveller time to relax and / or shop and visit places of interest not included in the tour.

RETAIL AGENTS

An agent who sells his individual travel services, e.g., accommodation, transportation, insurance etc., to the visitors.

RETAILERS

Businesses whose sales come primarily from retailing.

RETAILING

All activities involved in selling goods or services directly to final consumers, for their personal non business use.

The sale directed to the ultimate consumers, distinguished from wholesaling. The selling of relatively large quantities of products to those who resell (the retailers).

RETURN SUBJOURNEY

Part of a journey wherein travel is from a point/country and return thereto and for which the fare is assessed as a single pricing unit using half-RT fares: RT/CT/NOJ and special fare OJ returning to the same or another country.

REVALIDATION STICKER

Official notice affixed to a flight coupon to indicate that a new reservation has been made.

REVALIDATION

Authorized stamping or writing upon the passenger ticket evidencing that it has been officially altered by the carrier.

REVENUE MANAGEMENT

Maximisation of profits from every flight and route network. Involves asking the question: How to determine how many seats should be reserved for each fare type in order to maximize revenue from each flight?

REVENUE PASSENGER KILOMETER (RPK)

A measure of passenger traffic that is calculated by multiplying the number of paying passengers by the number of kilometers flown during a flight leg (i.e., segment of flight).

REVIEW DATES

A periodic evaluation of the progress of the sale and promotion of a group combined with attendant cabin utilization.

RNAV

Acronym for radio navigation.

RNP

Acronym for required navigation performance.

ROAD SHOW

Road shows are promotional events which showcase the products and services of a company in various places. The road shows have become the benchmark in the travel industry. It is a one stop shop for the most sought after/popular travel offers/products. The road shows aim at showcasing the viability of company / organization's business. It offers a holistic planning opportunity. Partners in the travel trade roadshow include representatives from the national tourism organizations, state and foreign countries tourism boards, airlines, travel agents and tour operators, cruise and rail companies. An opportunity is provided to all to get best possible deals.

ROCK CLIMBING

Climbing straight flat rock. The activity can be performed in areas which have rock formation.

ROLE

The activities that a person is expected to perform according to the persons around him or her.

ROLL-ON/ ROLL-OFF BOATS (RO RO)

Acronym for Roll-on/ Roll-off boats, Ferries designed for vehicle transport with the same entrance and exit at both ends of the boat, allowing vehicles to roll on and off with maximum efficiency.

ROLL

The movement of the plane that occurs when one wingtip dips lower than the other.

ROOM SERVICE

Food and beverages served in the sleeping rooms of the guests.

ROOM, BLOCK

A group of rooms or meeting space usually reserved through travel agents or wholesalers. These are held with a deposit.

ROOM, NIGHT

One overnight stay per person per room, i.e., two persons in one room for one night = two room nights.

ROOM, SINGLE

A room designed for one person; some rooms will have only one single bed while most will have twin (twin beds).

ROUND THE WORLD

Travel from a point and return thereto which involves only one crossing of the Atlantic Ocean and only one crossing of the Pacific Ocean.

ROUND TRIP

A Round Trip (RT) is travel entirely by air from a point to another point and return to the point of origin comprising two half round trip fare components only, for which the applicable half round trip for each component, measured from the point of unit origin is the same for the routing travelled.

ROUTE FARE, DIRECT

The fare over the direct route between two points.

ROUTE, DIRECT

The shortest all year route operated by an TC Member in both directions between ticketed points at which it exercises traffic rights.

ROUTINE RESPONSE BEHAVIOUR

Buying behaviour in cases in which buyers face simple buying decisions for low-cost, low-involvement, frequently purchased items in familiar product classes. Buyers do not give much thought, search, or time to the purchase.

RUDDER

The hinged part of the vertical stabilizer that is used to deflect the tail to the left and right as viewed from the front of the fuselage.

RUNNING LIGHTS

There lights (green on starboard side, red on portside and white at the top of the mast) are required by international law to be lighted when the ship is in motion between sunset and sunrise.

RUNWAY

The specially prepared concrete surface used for take-off and landing, usually aligned so aircraft can take off into the wind.

RURAL TOURISM

Rural tourism is "any form of tourism that showcases the rural life, art, culture and heritage at rural locations, thereby benefiting the local community economically and socially, as well as enabling interaction between the tourists and the local community for a more enriching tourism experience. It is any activity that takes place in the countryside.It is multifaceted and may entail farm or agricultural tourism and is experience oriented.The locations are predominantly in natural environment, and are based on preservation of Culture, heritage and traditions.

Visiting the rural / farm areas showcasing that ethnic arts, crafts, culture and lifestyle in its traditional settings. Rural tourism is assuming importance in those countries, which have strong agricultural base.

S

SAFETY MANAGEMENT SYSTEM

A set of organizational measures and procedures designed to manage safety at an aerodrome. It exists to ensure compliance with all safety requirements and to achieve continuous improvements in safety performance. It included a description of the measures undertaken by the airport for the promotion of safety and accident prevention.

SAFETY OVERSIGHT AUDIT (SOA) PROGRAMME

A universal programme established by ICAO in 1998 to conduct regular safety audits of the civil aviation authorities in different countries in relation to personnel licensing, operation of aircraft, and airworthiness.

SAFETY, AVIATION

Refers to the efforts that are taken to ensure airplanes are free from factors that may lead to injury or loss.

SAILING, PARA

Winching or towing a parachutist to a height of a few hundred feet in the air and then descending by means of a parachute.

SALES BLITZ

A concentrated burst of sales activity within a specific area by a group of sales people, such as many persons in one territory.

SALES LETTER

A direct mail material through which an attempt is made to gain agreement or favourable action towards a product.

SALES-FORCE PROMOTION

Sales promotion designed to motivate the sales force and make sales force selling efforts more effective, including bonuses, contests, and sales rallies.

SALES

Any process involving getting rid of what you have.

SAMPLE

A segment of population selected for marketing research to represent the population as a whole. It is a Offer of a trial amount of a product to consumers.

SANCTUARY, WILDLIFE

In a wildlife sanctuary, protection is only given to the fauna and operations like harvesting of timber, collection of minor forest products and private ownership rights are permitted so long as they do not interfere with the well being of the animals.

SAND BOARDING

This is like snowboarding but is done on sand instead. The rider stands on a board and cascades down a sand dune. The feet are either strapped on to the board or in more thrilling situation just placed on it. It is popular sport in South Africa, UAE and Australia.

SARP

Acronym for Standards and Recommended Practices.

SATISFACTION, CUSTOMER

Customer satisfaction with a purchase depends on the product's performance relative to a buyer's expectations. If performance matches expectations, the consumer is satisfied.

SAUNA

A steam bath available at spa and a health Centre. The water available has medicinal values and is considered to be curative.

SCANNER

An external device used to copy a paper or book image into an electronic format.

SCHEDULE, FLIGHT

The timetable showing all flights of an airline, and their scheduled departure and arrival times.

An air transport service that operates according to a pre-planned timetable on a specified licensed routes. The services are to operate regardless of number of passengers booked.

SCHEDULED FLIGHTS

Typically take place using predetermined routes according to a planned timetable.

SCHEDULING, CREW

The department responsible for projecting and scheduling all trips for the crew. Often involves two areas of responsibility: Crew Planning, which organizes all advance schedules, including training, vacation and hotel needs and Crew Scheduling, which handles responsibilities such as, ensuring appropriate staffing, coverage and assignments to reserve, or on call flight attendants.

SCHEME, AIRSPACE CLASSIFICATION

Adopted by ICAO in 1990, this scheme categories airspace into seven classes. Each is identified by a letter from A to G. The classes are fundamentally defined in terms of flight rules and interactions between aircraft and Air Traffic

Control (ATC). Regulations specify the type of flight permitted (IFR, VFR, or SVFER- Special flight Rules) and the type of air traffic control service provided for each.

SCHENGEN VISA

The word Schengen originates from a small town in Luxembourg. In the year 1985, Seven European Union Countries signed a treaty to end internal border check points and controls. Later, more countries joined and currently there are 24. Alphabetically Austria, Belgium, Czech Republic, Denmark, Estonia, Finland, France, Greece, Hungary, Iceland, Italy, Latvia, Lithuania, Luxembourg, Malta, Netherlands, Norway, Poland, Portugal, Slovakia, Slovenia, Spain, Sweden. All the countries except Norway and Iceland are members of European Union.

SCUBA DIVING

The activity of giving underwater carrying. Scuba stands for self contained underwater breathing apparatus. This consists of a cylinder of compressed air and tube through which one breathes the air (oxygen). A scuba diver also wear a diving suit while in ordinary diving no such special equipment is used by the diver. Ordinary diving is for a very short period (because of no oxygen supply) as compared to scuba diving.

SCUBA

Scuba stands for Self Contained Underwater Breathing Apparatus. The word has become an adjective to describe the popular aquatic sport scuba diving. By carrying a source of compressed air, the scuba diver is able to stay underwater longer than with the simple breath – holding techniques used in snorkeling.

SEAMLESS CONNECTIVITY

The ability to make direct reservations electronically without interfacing with another party.

SEARCH ENGINE

Search engines are applications that facilitate searching for information on the WWW. They can search by a key word or a concept.

SEARCH, INFORMATION

The stage of the buyer decision process in which a consumer is aroused to search for more information; the consumer may simply have heightened attention or may go into active information search.

SEASON, HIGH

Time of year when tourist traffic and rates are usually the highest because demand is highest.

SEASON

A consistent pattern of sales movements within the year.

SEASONAL RATES

Variations in prices for the same service, depending upon the time of the year.

SEASONALITY

All types and forms of tourism has a seasonality factor. There are peak seasons, lean or shoulder seasons and off seasons in almost every destination or in tourist generating market. Seasonality refers to variations in the demand for tourism products which makes it difficult for prodders of tourism products and services to sustain business all the year round. The demand for tourism products such as transportation, accommodation etc.is seasonal in nature.

SECOND/LATE SEATING

The later of two mealtimes in the ship's dining room.

SECONDARY DATA COLLECTION (TOURISM DATA)

Secondary data or desk research refers to information available from the secondary sources. The researcher becomes the secondary user of the data. Secondary data can be obtained from the international tourism organizations such as UNWTO, IATA, ICAO, WTTC, , PATA etc. which regularly publish statistical information. The information can also be obtained from national tourism boards, airlines and hotel companies. All published sources of data constitute secondary research.

SECONDARY DATA

Information that already exists somewhere, having been collected for another purpose.

SECURITY, AVIATION

A combination of measures and human and material resources intended to safeguard civil aviation against acts of unlawful interference.

SEGMENTATION ANALYSIS

The process of examining various sub markets and selecting those most appropriate for a company.

SEGMENTATION, MARKET

The analysis, planning, implementation and control of programs designed to create, build and maintain beneficial exchanges with target buyers for the purpose of achieving organizational objectives.

SEGMENTATION, BEHAVIOUR

Dividing a market into groups based on consumers' knowledge, attitude, use, or response to a product.

SEGMENTATION, BENEFIT

Dividing the market into groups according to the different benefits that consumers seek from the product.

SEGMENTATION, DEMOGRAPHIC

Dividing the market into groups based on demographic variables such as age, gender, family, size family life cycle, occupation, income, education, religion, race and nationality.

SEGMENTATION, INCOME

Dividing the market into different income groups.

SEGMENTATION, PSYCHOGRAPHIC

Dividing the market into different groups based on social class, lifestyle, or personality characteristics.

SEGMENT

Segment is a portion or a section of an itinerary and includes travel from one point to another. The itineraries have air segments, surface segments, outbound segments and return segments.

SELF-CATERING ACCOMMODATION

This type of accommodation describes fully furnished and equipped holiday accommodation in mainly privately owned apartment and houses where tourist may cater for themselves. A certain amount of servicing such as cleaning and maintenance is provided.

SELLING CONCEPT

The idea that consumers will not buy enough of an organization's products unless the organization undertakes a large selling a promotion effort.

SELLING, PERSONAL

Oral presentation in a conversation with one or more prospective purchasers for the purpose of making sales.

SEPARATION

The action of air traffic controllers undertaken to ensure that airplanes flying maintain minimum distances from other airplanes, thus reducing the likelihood of collisions. In- flight collisions are avoided by ensuring that horizontal and vertical separation is maintained between aircraft.

SERVICE LEVEL AGREEMENT (SLA)

A service Level Agreement (SLA) is a negotiated agreement between two parties where one is the customer and the other is the service provider. This can be legally binding formal or informal contract. The SLA records a common understanding about services, priorities, responsibilities, guarantees, and warranties.Service level agreements by nature are "output" based–the result of the service as received by the customer is the result of the agreement.

SERVICE CHARGES

These are percentage of guest hotel bill and vary between 10 percent and 15 percent assessed as tips (gratuities) to the hotel staff for the services rendered by them. Some hotels include a service charge in the bill itself.

SERVICE CULTURE

A system of values and beliefs in an organization that reinforces the idea that providing the customer with quality service is the principal concern of the business.

SERVICE INSEPARABILITY

A major characteristic of service; they are produced and consumed at the same time and cannot be separated from their providers whether the providers are people or machines.

SERVICE INTANGIBILITY

A major characteristic of services; they cannot be seen, tested, felt, heard or smelled before they are bought.

SERVICE PERISHABILITY

A major characteristics of services; they cannot be stored for later safe or use.

SERVICE QUALITY

From the provider's perspective, the degree to which the service's features conform to the organization's specifications and requirements; from the customer's perspective, how well the service meets or exceeds expectations and how much satisfaction it provides.

SERVICE RECOVERY

The effort of an organization to win back customers goodwill once it has been lost due to service failure.

SERVICE VARIABILITY

A major characteristic of services and their quality may vary greatly, depending on who provides them and when, where and how they are provided.

SERVICE, CUSTOMER

All customer provider interactions other than proactive selling and the core product delivery that facilitate the organizations relationship with its customers.

SERVICE, SHUTTLE

Complimentary transport provided from hotel to the airport. In some cases it may also be provided from airport to the hotel.

SERVICE

Any activity, benefit or satisfaction that is offered for sale. It is essentially intangible and does not result in the ownership of anything. Its production may or may not be tied to a physical product.

SERVICED ACCOMMODATION

Accommodation such as hotels, guest houses, motels, resorts etc. that provide guest services. The facilities available in these establishments include reception, meals, porters, laundry, parking and entertainment.

SERVICES, ALERTING

The Air Navigation Service that notifies appropriate organizations when an airplane is missing or in trouble.

SERVICES, COMPLIMENTARY

Services that accompany a core product and support its acquisition usage and / or disposition.

SETTING, CYBERSPACE

Any Web site on the Internet, subject to all of the principles and concepts that apply to managing the tangible evidence of a conventional service environment.

SHARING, CODE

This enables a passengers to fly a segment of their trip on an airplane other than the airplane that sold the ticket for the flight.

SHIP, CARGO

A vessel used to transport goods and in certain cases passengers as well.

SHOP, BUCKET

An unlicensed retailer, bound by no travel; association, buys seats in bulk from airline at a massive discount and sells them individually to the public.

SHOPPING, ELECTRONIC

Direct marketing through a two-way system that links consumers with the seller's computerized catalog by cable or telephone lines.

SHORE EXCURSION

Tours at ports of call for which an extra charge is usually applied.

SHORT HAUL TRAVEL

A air travel of less than four hour's duration.

SHOULDER SEASON

Time of the year between the high and off-season during which intermediate fares are applied.

SHUTTLE SERVICE

Complimentary transport provided from hotel to the airport. In some cases it may also be provided from airport to the hotel.

SIDE TRIP

Travel from and/or to an enroute point of a fare component.

SIDELINE CITY

To city in the fares list.

SINGLE OCCUPANCY

Sole occupancy of a cabin that is designed to accommodate two or more passengers, in which instance a premium is ordinarily charged.

SINGLE ROOM

A room designed for one person; some rooms will have only one single bed while most will have twin (twin beds).

SINGLE SUPPLEMENT

An additional charge paid by a tour participant who is travelling alone and chooses to occupy a double occupancy accommodation.

SITA

A global communication network set up to handle inter-airline message transmission in Europe. In the USA the system is known as the AIRINC network.

SITE PLANNING

Site planning and design is a process that involves in a integrated way the issues of land use, human circulation, structures, facilities and utilities within the natural and human environment. In order to ensure harmony between tourism development, and environmental protection, it is indispensable to apply sensitive design of infrastructure, master site planning, ecologically and socially conscious site design and landscaping. The site planning and design for any tourism facility must be, first of all, an instrument that safeguards the sustainability conservation of the surrounding natural and cultural heritage.

SITE, CAMPING

A place providing simple and inexpensive shelter to travellers. The site provides wayside amenities for tourists travelling by long distance coach tours and self-driven cars.

SITUATIONAL AWARENESS

Can be described as a person's state of knowledge or mental perception of the situation around him or her.

SKIING, WATER

A sport practiced by being towed behind a motorboat or any large water body.

SKY DIVING

Also known as free fall. A skydiver jumps of an aircraft or balloon at a much greater height without deploying his parachute initially and opens it after some interval at a predetermined height.

SLATS

Located at the front of the wings, slats are used at takeoff and landing to produce additional force.

SLEEPERS

Sleeping cars consisting of a private bedroom with accommodation for one or two persons. Sheets, pillows and blankets are included in the cost of a ticket.

SMOKING

Rooms where tobacco can be smoked. Non-smoking rooms prohibit tobacco use.

SNORKELING

Snorkeling (British spelling: snorkeling) is the practice of swimming on or through a body of water while equipped with a diving mask, a shaped tube called a snorkel, and usually swim ins. In cooler waters, a wetsuit may also be worn. Using this equipment allows the snorkeler to observe underwater attractions for extended periods of time with relatively little effort.

It is a popular recreational activity, particularly at tropical resort and scuba diving locations. Snorkeling is also employed by scuba divers when on the surface, and search and rescue teams may snorkel as part of a water-based search.

The primary attraction of snorkeling is the opportunity to observe underwater life in a natural setting without the complicated equipment and training required for scuba diving, and without the exhaled bubbles of scuba-diving equipment. Snorkeling is also a means to an end in popular sports such as underwater hockey, underwater ice hockey, underwater rugby and spearfishing.

SOCIAL CLASSES

Relatively permanent and ordered divisions in a society whose members share similar values, interests, and behaviours.

SOCIAL TOURISM

All the relations and phenomenon resulting from the accession to tourism of low income groups made possible or facilitated by specific social measures. It is the type of tourism practiced by those who otherwise would not be able to meet the cost without social intervention; i.e. without the assistance of an association to which the individual belongs.

SOCIETAL MARKETING CONCEPT

The idea that an organization should determine the needs, wants, and interests of target markets and deliver the desired satisfactions more effectively and efficiently than competitors in a way that maintains or improves the consumer's and society's well-being.

SOCIO CULTURAL IMPACTS

The impacts or effects of tourism on the social and cultural traditions of the host community. The impacts may be both positive or negative, good or bad depending upon the management of a destination.

SOFTWARE, APPLICATIONS

Applications software is the programme designed for a specific task, for example, word processing, data base management, etc.

SOFTWARE

Software is the computer programme or set of instructions that is installed on a computer in order to allow it to perform certain functions.

SOUTH EAST ASIAN ASSOCIATION FOR REGIONAL COOPERATION (SAARC)

It compromises the seven nations of South Asia: Bangladesh, Bhutan, India, Maldives, Nepal, Pakistan and Sri Lanka; founded as South Asia Regional Cooperation (SARC) organization at a meeting of foreign ministers in New Delhi on August 1-2, 1983; a second organizational meeting of foreign ministers held in Thimphu in May 1985: inaugural meeting of heads of state and government in Dhaka on December 7-8, 1985. The goal is to effect economic, technical, cultural and tourism cooperation and to provide a forum for discussions of South Asia political problems.

SPA

A resort providing therapeutic baths and ayurvedic treatment having or exhibiting powers: a therapeutic agent, therapeutic exercises. A resort area having mineral springs.

SPACE TOURISM

Space tourism involves sending passengers on suborbital flights that offer a brief experience of weightlessness and a thrilling view of the earth below.

Space tourism covers travel to the earth's orbit and sub-orbit, travel to planets beyond the earth's orbit to Mars. It also covers earth-based simulated experiences at NASA centre and entertainment based experiences.It will give the space tourist the unique and thrilling experience of viewing the earth from outer space.

A recent phenomenon of space travel by individuals for the purposes of personal pleasure. The primary attractions of space tourism are to have a feel of weightlessness as also unforgettable view of space and its wonders.

SPANNERS, BOUNDARY

The front-stage employees who link an organization with its customers.

SPECIAL FARE

Any fare other than a normal fare.

SPECIAL INTEREST TOURISM

Special interest travel is travel for people who are going somewhere because they have a particular interest that can be pursued in a particular region or at a particular destination.

Tourism that combines elements designed to appeal to those with certain narrow interests, also known as "niche tourism".

SPECIAL MEAL

Meals that meet dietary requirements. Passengers request special meals for religious reasons, health requirements or personal preferences and are ordered in advance of a flight. Some types of special meals include kosher, vegetarian or children's meals.

SPECIAL OLYMPICS

It is an international organization created to help people with physical disabilities to develop a sense of personal accomplishment through sports training and competition. Among their other activities, special Olympics conducts the special Olympic world games every four years.

SPECIALTIES, ADVERTISING

Useful articles imprinted with an advertiser's name given as gifts to consumers.

SPIRITUAL TOURISM

Also called Pilgrimage Tourism is one of the most popular form of the tourism since ancient times. It involves travel to religious places for spiritual benefit.

SPORTS TOURISM

Any kind of organized indoor or outdoor activity which people pursue for recreation and physical fitness. A form of tourism in which a person travel from place of his residence to a place where sporting activity is organized in order to either take part in or watch a sporting event. The sporting event could be local, national, regional and international.

STABILIZERS

The parts of the tail whose job is to provide stability for the aircraft, to keep it flying straight. The vertical stabilizer keeps the nose of the plane from swinging side to side, while the horizontal stabilizer prevents an up-and-down motion of the nose.

STAFF, BACK OFFICE

These are employees whose primary employment objective is to support the front line personnel who deliver a service.

STAGE, DECLINE

The product-life-cycle stage when a product's sales decline.

STAND, BELL

A portion of the lobby set aside for receiving luggage and distributing it to all the guests in their room.

STAND-BY PASSENGER

A passenger who does not have a confirmed reservation, but arrives at the airport with the hope of being accommodated at departure time. Non-revenue travellers are also considered stand by.

STAND-BY

A passenger who does not hold a confirmed reservation, but waits at the airport ready to undertake a journey, if a seat may be made available at the last minute.

STANDARD AIRWORTHINESS CERTIFICATE

A document that grants authorization to operate a civil aircraft in flight. The standard Airworthiness Certificate means that the aircraft conforms to its type design, and it is in safe operating condition for a safe flight.

STANDARD

A specification for physical characteristics or performance of a facility or a personnel, the uniform application of which is recognized as necessary for reasons of safety or regularity of international air navigation. Its application by all member states is mandatory.

Regular size sleeping rooms. The bedding might consist of one or two double beds.

STARBOARD

A term used to refer to the right side of the airplane. (Also referred to as aircraft right).

The right side of the ship when facing towards the bow (front).

STATISTICAL DEMAND ANALYSIS

A set of statistical procedures used to discover the most

important real factors affecting sales and their relative influence.

STATUS

The general esteem given to a role by society.

STEP-ON GUIDES

Step-On guides are specialized tour guides who join the tour briefly to conduct a portion of the tour, such as art gallery or a museum.

STERN

The extreme rear of the ship or toward the rear.

STOLEN DOCUMENT

An Accountable Traffic Document which was removed from the possession of its lawful custodian as a result of a break-in, burglary, robbery or theft, or which has been fraudulently obtained from a traffic document distributor.

STOPOVER

When a passenger arrives at an intermediate point and is not scheduled to depart within 24 hours of arrival.

STRATEGIC RELATIONSHIP

An agreement between two or more enterprises to conduct specified business processes in a joint manner. Usually related to technology development and / or marketing or distribution efforts

STRATEGIC ALLIANCE

A strategic alliance is a form of relationship between two or more parties to pursue a set of agreed upon goals to meet the critical business need. It is a collaborative agreement between two companies designed to achieve some strategic goal. Strategic alliances include international Licensing agreements, management contracts, and joint ventures as specific cases.

Relationship between independent parties that agree to co-operate and still retain their separate identities. For instance strategic alliances between airlines for code share or frequent fliers programmes.

Relationships between independent parties that agree to co-operate but still retain separate identities.

STRATEGIC BUSINESS UNITS (SBUs)

A single business or collection or related businesses that can be planned separately from the rest of the company.

SUB-CULTURE

A group of people with shared value systems based on common life experience and situations.

SUBSTANTIALITY

The degree to which a market segment is large or profitable enough.

SUGGESTED ITINERARY

A preliminary itinerary provided by tour operations for the travellers consideration. This itinerary generally shows routing and approximate times as well as recommended hotels and suggested sight-seeing excursions, and spells out the conditions under which these services will be provided.

SUITE

A combination of connecting rooms.

Consists of two or more rooms, typically a living and sleeping room. A suite may have more than one bedroom or extra rooms such as kitchenette or conference room.

SUPERIOR

Sleeping room may include double, queen–size or king–size bed.

SUPPLEMENT, SINGLE

An additional charge paid by a tour participant who is travelling alone and chooses to occupy a double occupancy accommodation.

SUPPLEMENTARY ACCOMMODATION

Various types of accommodation units other than the conventional hotel type. It includes accommodation for travellers in motels, youth hostels, camping sites etc. and is normally used by budget tourists.

SUPPLEMENTARY MOTIVATORS

Motivators other than base salary and commission, such as sales contests.

SUPPLIER SEARCH

The stage of the industrial buying process in which a buyer tries to find the best vendors.

SUPPLIER SELECTION

The stage of the industrial buying process in which a buyer receives proposals and selects a supplier or suppliers.

SUPPLIER

A company which provides the actual components of travel. Components may include transfer, accommodation, sight-seeing etc.

SUPPLIERS

Firms and individuals that provide the resources needed

by a company and its competitors to produce goods and services.

SURFACE SECTOR

A sector not travelled by air but by land or sea. An imbedded surface sector means a domestic or international surface sector within a fare component, but not to or from a fare construction point. A fare construction surface sector means either the origin or the termination point of a domestic or international surface sector is at a fare construction point, including the origin or destination of a pricing unit. A fare construction surface sector from the point of origin of a pricing unit is not permitted.

SURFING, WIND

A small surfboard with an attached sails used for sliding the surf on the sea. Directional control is achieved by shifting the sail position and body weight of the wind surfs.

SURFING

A sport where only a surfboard is used for riding the waves and surf on the seas. The control is achieved by body maneuver.

SURVEY RESEARCH

The gathering of primary data from the field by asking people questions about their knowledge, attitudes, preferences and buying behaviour.

SUSTAINABILITY

The sustainable development approach implies that the natural, cultural and other resources of tourism are conserved for continuous use in the future while still bringing benefit to the present society.

SUSTAINABLE DEVELOPMENT

A process of developing land, cities, business, and communities, that "meets the needs of the present without compromising the ability of future generations to meet their own needs".

SUSTAINABLE TOURISM

Sustainable tourism is envisaged as leading to management of all resources in such a way that economic, social and aesthetic needs can be fulfilled while maintaining cultural integrity, essential ecological processes, biological diversity and life support systems.The term is also used to describe all form of long term tourism which are in harmony with their physical, social and cultural environment and meet the present needs as well as the future generation needs.

Tourism operations that seek to preserve the natural, physical and socio-cultural environments of host destination, thereby ensuring that tourists continue to be attracted.

SWATH

Acronym for Small Water plane Area Twin Hull. A new ferry design with hydrofoil features but improved stability and efficiency.

SLOPS

Crew store managed by volunteer crew members offering everything from snacks and toiletries to uniforms and cover alls.

SECTION 7: T

Travel agent, tourist product, tourist charter, tourist facilities, tours and tour operations, tourism organizations, ticketing, trade promotions, theme parks, tourism satellite account and miscellaneous.

TABLE D' HôTE

A fixed price meal offered daily in a hotel.

TAG, BAGGAGE

A document indicating the passengers name and address that is attached to the luggage as means of identification.

TAKE OFF

The act of the aircraft lifting from the runway.

TANGIBLE PRODUCT

The product which can be seen and touched before purchase.

TARGET MARKET

A set of buyers sharing common needs or characteristics that a company decides to serve.

TARGET

A goal or point at which you aim selling a product as per the target.In other words trying to complete the target.

TARIFF

The published fares, rates, charges and or related conditions of carriage of a carrier.

TAVERN

A place of business where people gather to drink alcoholic beverages and, more than likely, also be served food, though not licensed to put up guests. The word derives from the Latin taberna and the Greek /taverna, whose original meaning was a shed or workshop. The distinction of a tavern from an inn, bar or pub varies by location, in some places being identical and in others being distinguished by traditions or by legal license. In Renaissance England, a tavern was distinguished from a public house by dint of being run as a private enterprise, where drinkers were "guests" rather than members of the public.

TAX

Charge levied on transportation documents or hotel bills.

TAXI

The movement of an aircraft on the ground while operating under its own power.

TEAM SALES

Multiperson involvement in the sales process.

TECHNICAL QUALITY

The quality of the core product that a guest receives in a transaction. In a hotel room; in a restaurant.

TECHNOLOGICAL ENVIRONMENT

Forces that create new technologies, in turn creating new product and market opportunities.

TELE MARKETING

Using the telephone to sell directly to consumers.

TENDER

A small boat used to transport people and supplies to and from a ship at anchor. Most large ships carry their own tenders, which are maintained as lifeboats in the case of an emergency.

TERMINAL BUILDING

A building at the airport where passengers check-in, depart or arrive from a flight.

TERMINAL CONTROL AREA

A block of airspace of cylindrical or irregular shape, located at intersections of several airways, and typically situated at high-density traffic areas near one or more busy airports. The block extends from at least 200m above the ground to an altitude determined by local traffic conditions and by the airspace structure above it. Its lateral dimensions depend on the amount and density of traffic to be handled.

TERMINAL

Area at an airport where the formalities for departing and arriving passengers take place.

TERMINAL

Part of the airport which is divided into arrival and departure sections. These sections can be superimposed on top of one another, if it is a multi-story terminal, or are located at their ends of the terminal building, if it is not. These are the general public access areas and, in more modern international airports, they also provide amenities such as stores, bars, restaurants, and banks or currency exchange services and travel insurance vendors.

TERRITORY-STRUCTURED SALES FORCE

A sales force structured according to the geographical location of the area.

TEST MARKETING

The stage of new-product development in which a product and marketing programme are tested in more realistic market settings.

THANK YOU!

Regardless of the language, an effective salutation to show appreciation to a client or prospect.

THEME PARK

A theme park is a special type of tourism attraction which is not necessarily related to the natural or cultural resources of a destination. The theme parks are oriented to a particular themes such as history, futurism, adventure, flora and fauna, wild life, cuisine, unusual geographical places, space or combination of all to offer the visitors an unforgettable experience. Theme parks are generally profit making business and have goals that are primarily profit driven and provide income to the owners or shareholders. The theme parks not only attract tourists but also a large number of day visitors as also local population.

THROTTLE

A device used by the pilot to control the engine's power and speed.

THROUGH FARE

A fare applicable for travel between two consecutive fare construction points via an intermediate point(s).

THROUGH PASSENGER

A person continuing on through an intermediate stop to a further destination.

THROW-AWAYS

Features of a tour that a client purchases but deliberately intends not to use.

THRUST

The force that opposes drag and moves the plane forward. The plane's engines or propeller create this thrust.

TICKET

A document representing the contract of carriage concluded between the company and the passenger as well as the passenger's receipt for the money paid.

TICKET ON DEPARTURE (TOD)

A procedure by which a travel agent makes special arrangements for a passenger's ticket to be issued by airlines staff at the departure airport.

TICKET, AUTOMATED

A form of passenger ticket and baggage check designed for issue in various printing devices for which data is computer generated.

TICKET, CONJUNCTION

A ticket issued to a passenger concurrently with another ticket(s) which together is considered a single contract of carriage.

TICKET, OPEN

A ticket which has been issued for a particular journey but on which a specific date has yet to be entered.

TICKETED POINT MILEAGE (TPM)

Distance between pairs of points published in the TPM manual using nonstop sector mileage.

TICKETING, ELECTRONIC (ET)

A new means of issuing tickets through electronic means (i.e., through the Internet and the use of self-service kiosks).

TIME-SERIES ANALYSIS

Consists of breaking down original sales into four components-trends, cycle, season, and erratic components- and then recombining these components to produce the sales forecast.

TIMETABLE

Specific dates to accomplish strategies and tactics.

TOTAL COSTS

The sum of the fixed and variable costs for any given level of production.

TOTAL CUSTOMER COST

The costs to a customer which include money, time and energy costs.

TOTAL CUSTOMER VALUE

A customer derives value from the core products, the service delivery system, and the company's image. These components make up total customer value.

TOUR BASING FARE

A reduced round trip fare available on specified dates, and between specified times, only to those passengers who purchase pre-planned, pre-paid tour arrangements from an agent prior to their departure.

TOUR CONDUCTOR

Person employed to escort members of a tourist group for the entire journey. Also called Leader, Escort, and Courier.

TOUR OPERATOR

A person or business entity that is responsible for the actual implementation and operation of the tour with the tour participants.

A travel organization that puts together inclusive tours. It buys the components (travel, accommodation, transfers) from principals and sells the complete package for an inclusive price. A tour operator may use travel agents or sell direct to tourists.

TOUR OPERATORS

The companies which operate all inclusive package tours. They do this by contracting with transport companies for seats to destinations and accommodation provides for beds, meals or other facilities at the resort / destination.

TOUR RETAILER

A person or business entity that buys the tour products from the tour wholesaler either at a net cost or on a commission basis, and sells these products to the general public.

TOUR WHOLESALER

A person or a business entity that obtains the components of the tour such as transportation, accommodation, attractions and sightseeing and packages them together, in the form of a tour, for sale to the tour retailer.

TOUR, INDEPENDENT

A tour where participants travel independently without an accompanying group or tour guide.

TOUR, CONDUCTED

A pre-paid, pre -arranged vacation in which a group of people travel together under the guideline of a tour leader who stays with them from the start to the end of the trip. Also referred to as an "escorted tour".

TOUR, ESCORT

A tour accompanied by a professional Tour Escort also called Tour Manager.

TOUR, GUARANTEED

A tour which is guaranteed to operate unless cancelled 60 days prior to departure. In the event of cancellation within 60 days of the departure date, full commission is paid to agents of sold clients.

TOUR, GUIDED

A tour conducted only by local city guilds.

TOUR, HOSTED

A tour where participants have an opportunity to travel independently, but also to receive guidance and assistance from a host at each of the tour's destinations.

TOUR, INCLUSIVE

A prearranged combination of air transportation and surface arrangements other than solely public transports.

TOUR, MOTOR COACH

A tour that utilizes motor coaches or buses to move tourists from one destination to another and to visit sight seeing attractions along the way. This type of tour gives ample opportunity for observing country / city sights.

TOUR, RAIL

A tour in which primary mode of transport during the tour is by train.

TOUR

Any form of travel from place to place, with multiple features that can be packaged and sold as a single unit.

TOURISM FORECASTING

Forecasting is the art of estimating future demand by anticipating what buyers are likely to do under a given set of conditions. Tourism managers need to base their decisions on certain assumptions such as behaviour pattern of customers, competitors strategies, seasonal variations etc.Forecasting helps manager.

TOURISM SATELLITE ACCOUNT

Tourism Satellite Account is a system of accounting at national or regional level which reveals the total direct impact of tourism on the economy.

TOURISM

A stay of one or more nights away from home for holiday, visits to friends or relatives, business conferences or any other purpose, except such things as boarding, education or semi-permanent employment.

TOURISM ACCOUNT

The way in which a country records the income from tourist arrivals and the expenditure by its own nationals on overseas tourism. The difference between these two accounts is known as the tourism balance.

TOURISM BALANCE

The economic difference between a country's receipts from incoming tourists and expenditure by its residents on outgoing tourism. The balance is said to be positive if receipts are greater than expenditure and negative if the opposite is true.

TOURISM CIRCUIT

A combination or multiple chain of destinations marketed as one product. Circuits offer a variety of attractions to tourists which otherwise are not possible to experience.

TOURISM FACILITIES

Facilities which include accommodation like hotels, boarding house, guest houses, youth hostels, resorts, camping sites etc. These also include recreational and sport facilities of great variety and also all the necessary infrastructure like transportation and utility.

TOURISM INCOME MULTIPLIER

The idea that tourism revenue is recycled within the host community as wages local purchases or investment in infrastructure, thereby multiplying its value. The concept of the multiplier is based on the recognition of the interdependence of trading organizations within a community. The amount of leakage from the local economy will affect the value of the multiplier.

TOURISM POLICY

Guidelines and decisions designed to assist the tourism industry in meeting objectives and goals. Tourism policy usually result from the actions of the government's various agencies and organizations.

TOURISM RESEARCH

Investigations with various aspects of tourism. The main objective of tourism research is to find out how people travel, when they travel, where they travel and why they travel. The areas like travel demand, domestic and international tourism, transportation, accommodation, planning etc. are covered in the research. The findings of the research become the base for planning and implementation of various programmes connected with tourism.

TOURISM, NICHE

Tourism that combines elements designed to appeal those with certain narrow or special interest.

TOURISM, ADVENTURE

Type of niche tourism involving exploration or travel to remote areas where the traveller should expect the unexpected.

TOURISM, ALTERNATIVE

A form of tourism that advocates smaller scale and limited tourism in terms of numbers of tourists involved and the dimension of tourism development. It is also called Green Tourism or Responsible Tourism.

TOURISM, BEACH

A coastal oriented tourism utilizing the aesthetic and environmental value of the beaches. It combines water and land resources usage.

TOURISM, BUSINESS

Business tourism is concerned with people travelling for purposes, which are related to their work. As such it represents the oldest forms of tourism, man having travelled for this purpose of trade, since very early times in the history.

TOURISM, CULTURAL

A form of tourism in which the culture and traditions of the region is the main attraction.

TOURISM, DOMESTIC

Tourism that does not entail visits outside the country's national boundaries by its citizen. This may include holidays, short breaks and business journeys.

TOURISM, ETHNIC

Ethnic tourism involves travel for the purpose of observing the cultural expressions of lifestyles and customs of the indigenous people.This type of tourism focuses directly on local people, it involves direct contact with the authentic culture of the indigenous people.The tourists visit the local homes of the host community, observe and participate in their traditional rituals, ceremonies, festivals etc.

TOURISM, GREEN

A form of tourism that advocates smaller scale and limited tourism in terms of numbers of tourists involved and the dimension of tourism development. Also called alternative tourism or responsible tourism.

TOURISM, HEALTH

It is a movement of tourists into a country for the consumption of health related services in the host country.

TOURISM, INBOUND

From the point of view of a destination, this describes the tourists who arrive from another country. It is therefore, a form of international tourism contributing to the economy of the receiving nation.

TOURISM, ISLAND

Island Tourism is associated with a quite holiday in a island which gives feeling of remoteness or seclusion.

TOURISM, LEISURE

Tourism or travel for pleasure and relaxation as opposed to business. It can take place at home (domestic) or abroad (international) and for a variety of reasons.

TOURISM, MASS

Large scale movement of travellers and the development of a standardized product.

TOURISM, MEDICAL

Provision of cost effective private medical care in collaboration with the tourism industry for patients needing surgical and other forms of specialized treatment at an affordable price. It covers a broad spectrum of medical services. It mixes leisure and relaxation together with wellness and healthcare.

TOURISM, OUTBOUND

International tourism seen from the point of view of the originating country. Outbound tourism is a form of importation of services from abroad and such has a negative effect on that country's tourism account.

TOURISM, PRIVATE SECTOR

That sector of the tourism industry, which is planned, financed and operated by the privately owned organization. Most of the tourism business in the world such as hotels, car hire companies, amusement parks, entertainment centres, transport organizations, tourist attractions, travel agencies and tour operators are owned and operated by private sector.

TOURISM, PUBLIC SECTOR

Tourism organizations and enterprises funded by government and generally for the benefit of society as a whole are known as a tourist information office or a national tourist board. Majority of the National Tourism Organizations such as airlines, rail systems, airports, may also be publicly owned and managed. The provision of service to the general public is the main consideration rather than profit motive.

TOURISM, RESPONSIBLE

A form of tourism that advocates smaller scale and limited tourism in term of numbers of tourists involved and the dimension of tourism development. It is also called green tourism or alternative tourism.

TOURISM, RURAL

Visiting the rural / farm areas showcasing that ethnic arts, crafts, culture and lifestyle in its traditional settings. Rural tourism is assuming importance in those countries, which have strong agricultural base.

TOURISM, SOCIAL

All the relations and phenomenon resulting from the accession to tourism of low income groups made possible or facilitated by specific social measures. It is the type of tourism practiced by those who otherwise would not be able to meet the cost without social intervention; i.e. without the assistance of an association to which the individual belongs.

TOURISM, SPACE

A recent phenomenon of space travel by individuals for the purposes of personal pleasure. The primary attractions of space tourism are to have a feel of weightlessness as also unforgettable view of space and its wonders.

TOURISM, SPECIAL INTEREST

Special interest travel is travel for people who are going somewhere because they have a particular interest that can be pursued in a particular region or at a particular destination.

TOURISM, SPORTS

Any kind of organized indoor or outdoor activity which people pursue for recreation and physical fitness. A form of tourism in which a person travel from place of his residence to a place where sporting activity is organized in order to either take part in or watch a sporting event. The sporting event could be local, national, regional and international.

TOURISM, SUSTAINABLE

Tourism operations that seek to preserve the natural, physical and socio-cultural environments of host destination, thereby ensuring that tourists continue to be attracted.

TOURISM, YOUTH

A desire of young people to travel, which can be realized on a very large scale due to technical facilities and increase in standard of living in the wake of socialization and democratization.

TOURIST BOARD, NATIONAL

A government body set up to represent the tourism interests of a country. One of the key national tourist Boards function is to promote its country abroad to attract foreign tourists.

TOURIST CENTRE

A village or town with a definite concentration of tourist resources, material base and infrastructure of tourism development.

TOURIST CHARTER

A flight booked exclusively for the use of a specific group of tourists who generally belong to the same organization or who are being 'treated' to the flight by a single host.

TOURIST COMPLEX

A massive architectural installation specifically meant for infrastructure tourism.

TOURIST DOMESTIC

A local person who makes a tour, travelling from place to place for pleasure, business, family, mission, meeting etc. within the boundaries of the country.

TOURIST FLOW

Undisturbed and even movement of tourists from one country to another for the purpose of travelling for pleasure.

TOURIST GENERATING COUNTRY

The country of origin from where the tourists travel to other countries for a short period of time purely for the purpose of leisure or business as well as also meeting friends and relatives.

TOURIST LODGE

A small house providing temporary accommodation to a tourist. The accommodation provided is inexpensive as compared to a conventional hotel. The lodge may also offer meal.

TOURIST OBJECT

Any object from a natural, socio-economic or cultural – historical viewpoint which has some specific attractions for the tourists.

TOURIST ORGANIZATION, NATIONAL

The body responsible for the formulation and implementation of national tourist policy. It is the agency and instrument for the execution of the national governments responsibilities for the control, direction and promotion of tourism.

TOURIST PRODUCT

A sum total of a country's tourist attractions, infrastructure and tourist services which hopefully result in consumer satisfaction.

TOURIST RECEIVING COUNTRY

The destination country to which tourist travel.

TOURIST REGION

A branch of economic region with specific high dependence on natural man made attractions.

TOURIST VISA

A document issued or endorsed on a passport under the authority of the Government to a person visiting a particular country as a tourist.

TOURIST, CHARTER

A flight booked exclusively for use of a specific group of tourist who generally belong to the same organization or who are being "treated" to the flight by a single host.

TOURIST, DESTINATION

A tourist who terminates his journey at a particular country for the purpose of making a tour, travelling from place to place for pleasure.

TOURIST, DOMESTIC

A local person who makes a tour travelling from place to place for pleasure, business, mission, family, meeting etc. within the country.

TOURIST, INTERNATIONAL

A person who makes a tour travelling from place to place for pleasure to areas outside his home country.

TOURIST

A temporary visitor staying at least twenty hours in the country visited and the purpose of whose journey can be classified under one of the following heading (leisure, recreation, holiday, health, study, religion and sport business, family, mission, meetings).

TRADE PROMOTION

Sales promotion designed to gain reseller support and to improve reseller selling efforts, including discounts, allowance, free goods, cooperative advertising, push money, and conventions and trade shows.

TRADEMARK

A brand or part of a brand that is given legal protection. The trademark protects the seller's exclusive rights to use a brand name or brand mark.

TRAFFIC DOCUMENT, ACCOUNTABLE

Paper value ticket, a miscellaneous charges order, a multiple purpose document whether issued or blank (excluding electronic formats).

TRAFFIC DOCUMENT, STANDARD

A neutral BSP ticket, a miscellaneous charges order, a multiple purpose document whether issued or blank.

TRAFFIC DOCUMENT

Value documents issued manually, mechanically or electronically for air passenger transportation over the lines of the Airline and for related services, whether or not they bear a pre-printed individual airline identification.

TRAFFIC, DESTINATION

Persons (tourists) carried by transportation lines and terminating their journey at one particular place.

TRANSACTION

A trade between two parties that involves at least two things of value, agreed-upon conditions, a time of agreement, and a place of agreement.

TRANSATLANTIC

Crossing or spanning the Atlantic Ocean or on the other side of the Atlantic Ocean.

TRANSFER, CARGO

Cargo arriving at a point by one flight and continuing its journey by another flight of the same or a connecting carrier.

TRANSFER, INTERLINE

Transfer from the service of one carrier to the service of another carrier.

TRANSFER, ONLINE

Transfer from the service of one carrier to another service of the same carrier.

TRANSFER, PASSENGER

A passenger arriving on the flight and continuing his journey on another.

TRANSFER, TRAFFIC

Persons (tourists) carried by transportation lines and passing through a country en route to some other destination.

TRANSFERS

Any mode of transport that shuttles participants from their point of arrival, frequently an airport, to their first accommodation, typically a hotel.

TRANSFER

The service provided to travellers from the time they arrive in a destination until they depart in a given city. The service would include - taking them from airport, air terminal, pier, railway station or bus terminal to their hotel and vice versa, generally accompanied by the local representative of the other operator who plan and organize the tour.

TRANSIT PASSENGER

A person continuing on a flight through an intermediate (transit) stop, and is also referred to as a "through-passenger".

TRANSIT VISITOR

A visitor who is passing over or through a country en route to some other destination. Unlike destination tourist, he spends limited time and visits few places of tourist interest.

TRANSIT, CARGO

Cargo arriving at a point and departing therefrom by the same through flight.

TRANSIT, PASSENGER

A passenger continuing his journey in the same through flight.

TRANSITIONAL AUTOMATED TICKET (TAT)

Form of automated ticket, normally issued by airline offices and is a multi-copy carbonized ticket.

TRANSIT

Passengers who are temporarily located at a point between their departure and destination. This situation arises as a result of changeover from one flight to another which may require change of an aircraft and the terminal in certain cases.

TRANSPORT PLANES, COMMERCIAL

The large planes owned or leased by an airline company designed specifically to carry passengers and cargo (or just cargo). The smallest can carry from 20 to 100 passengers and the largest can carry several hundreds. Most of these planes are jet planes with two, three or four engines.

TRAVEL AGENT

A person, firm or corporation qualified to provide travel services including tours, cruises, transportation, hotel accommodation, meals, transfers, sight-seeing, insurance and all other elements of travel to the public. An important contributor to the airline industry, who is authorized to sell and issue airline tickets.

TRAVEL AND TOURISM

The travel industry is made up of industries that provide or facilitate temporary transportation for business or pleasure.

TRAVEL KIT

A sort of container which contains accessories or tools. Travel kit contains various types of material like folders, pamphlets, exhibit, presentation items, give-away etc. which help travel manager in organizing promotional activities. It is an aid which helps in promoting and projecting a organization's product. The contents of a kit however, vary depending on the area where it is to be used and also amount set-aside for the purpose.

TRAVEL MAGAZINE

A magazine which contains articles and other reading material devoted to travel and tourism. The main objective of a travel magazine is promotion of tourism. The contents are of value to both intended travellers also having interest in tourism

TRAVEL MARKETS

The areas which exist in populated localities whose individuals possess leisure, income and desire to visit areas foreign to their residence.

TRAVEL MISSION

Goodwill selling by a company as part of a broader group, such as an association establishing information booths at a travel show.

TRAVEL VOUCHER

Travel voucher is a all purpose voucher issued by a tour operator to cover the prepaid elements of a package tour such as meals, local transport and entrance fee for attractions. The voucher is given to the ground handling agent.

TRAVEL, BUSINESS

Business Travel is the act of travelling for purposes which are related to their work, like meetings, conferences and conventions on behalf of the corporate entity or business at its expense. Business travel is that category of tourism in which travellers visit distant destination within their own country or outside the country to conduct their business activities. This could involve attending meetings, participating in seminars; conferences and conventions as also trade fairs and exhibitions.

TREKKING

A journey across forest tracks or in the country side; which is still largely untouched by formal means of transportation.

TREND

The long-term, underlying pattern of growth or decline in sales resulting from basic changes in population, capital formation, and technology.

TURNDOWN

Provided free of charge at some hotels, this service includes removing the bedspread, turning down the bed linens, fluffing the pillows, drawing the curtains and often supplying a chocolate or other sweet dessert item.

TWIN BED

A room designed for two people with two beds (may also indicate a Twin Bed).

TWIN

A room designed for two people with two beds (may also indicate a Twin Bed).

SECTION 8: U & V

Up-selling, ticket up-gradation, unaccompanied baggage, united nations, unit cost, voice recorder, vouchers, variable cost, visa, visitor, and miscellaneous.

UNACCOMPANIED BAGGAGE

The baggage not carried on the same aircraft as that on which the passenger is carried.

UNACCOMPANIED MINOR (UM)

A child, up to the age of 12, who travels alone, not accompanied by an adult.

UNCONTROLLED AIRSPACE

The part of airspace in which pilots are responsible for making sure they keep sufficient distance from other airplanes.

UNDIFFERENTIATED MARKETING

A market-coverage strategy in which a firm decides to ignore market segment differences and go after the entire market with one market offer.

UNIT COSTS

A measure of operating costs, an important factor in determining airline profitability.

UNIT DESTINATION

The ultimate stopping place of a pricing unit.

UNIT ORIGIN

The initial starting point of a pricing unit.

UNITED NATIONS (UN)

The United Nations, or UN, is an international organization made up of 191 states established in 1945. Almost all countries are members. UN membership is open to all "peace-loving states" that accept the obligations of the UN Charter and, in the judgment of the organization, are able and willing to fulfil these obligations. The General Assembly determines admission upon recommendation of the Security Council. As of January 2005 there have been 191 members.

UNITED NATIONS EDUCATIONAL, SCIENTIFIC AND CULTURAL ORGANIZATION (UNESCO)

UNESCO is a specialized agency of the United Nations system established in 1946. The organizations main objective is to contribute to peace and security by promoting collaboration among the nations through education, science and culture in order to further universal respect for justice, for the rule of law and for the human rights and fundamental freedoms (Article 1 of UNESCO's Constitution).

UP-SELLING

Once you've closed the sale and secured a commitment from your client, activity directed towards providing your client with options to purchase upgraded accommodations, a better model of car, or some other better travel option.

UPGRADE

To move up to a higher standard of accommodation at little cost or on a complimentary basis.

USER

The person who consumes or uses a product or service.

VACATIONS

A person staying away from home for couple of nights on any one trip and may in some instances include tourist travelling for a combination of business and pleasure.

VALIDATION

The authorized stamping or writing upon the Passenger Ticket giving proof that it has been officially issued by the carrier.

VALUES

Refer to what is important to a company, which tasks should have the highest priority and which aspects of an employee's performance are most important.

VALUE

The combination of quality and price.

VARIABLE COSTS

All expenses that change according to the number of clients who take a tour.

VENUE

Where buyer and sellers meet to transact business.A display and sale of products or services to an invited audience or to the general public is organized with a aim of creating awareness and promoting products.

VERTICAL MARKETING SYSTEM (VMS)

A distribution channel structure in which producers, wholesalers and retainers act as a unified system; either one channel member owns the others, or has contracts with them, or has so much power that they all cooperate.

VERTICAL SEPARATION

The action undertaken by air traffic controllers requiring aircraft to operate at different levels expressed in terms of flight levels or altitudes.

VIEWDATA

The name of a computer system enabling travel agents to access the systems of tour operators and airlines in order to make reservations on behalf of clients. Similar to Global Distribution System (GDS).

VIP

Very important person or passenger, who usually requires extra attention and has special requests regarding their travel.

VISA TRANSIT

An endorsement on a passport which is issued to a tourist whose destination is somewhere else and is passing across. Such visitors passing through a country en-route to some other destinations are granted transit visa on production of a through ticket for the onward journey.

VISA, BIOMETRIC

It requires statistical analyses of biological observations and phenomenon. The process takes finger scans and a digital photograph as part of the visa application process. The process is to proof and protects that customers from identity brand. The unauthorized persons will not be able to access the biometric data and the data will not be used inappropriately.

VISA, ENTRY

An endorsement on passport issued to a person who wish to visit a country for purposes of business, employment, permanent residence, profession etc. Initially issued for a period of three months these are extendable to a further period of three months.

VISA, TOURIST

A document issued or endorsed on a passport under the authority of the Government to a person visiting a particular country as a tourist.

VISA, TOURIST

An endorsement on a passport issued to a person who wishes to visit a country as a tourist. The visa is effective for a period of three months. Tourists must arrive within six months of the date of issue of visa. The tourist can extend his stay for a further period of three months if he applies to the concerned authorities.

VISA

Visitor's intention to stay abroad. An endorsement on the passport issued by the representative of a government. The endorsement enables a person to travel to a country for which it is issued.

VISITING FRIENDS AND RELATIVE (VFR)

A form of tourism in which the main motivation is to stay with or near one's friends or relatives.

VISITOR PLANT

All accommodation, transport etc. points of interest in a destination area.

VISITOR, BUSINESS

A business visitor includes a person who visits a country to transact business, including attending meetings and briefing, fact finding, negotiating or making contacts with business to buy or sell goods or services. The list of typical business visitors also includes those visiting a country to purchase trade goods and those visiting for training in techniques and work practices, provided that the training is confined to observation, familiarization and classroom instructions.

VISITOR, DAY

A tourist who does not stay overnight at the destination. Also known as an excursionist

VISITOR, TRANSIT

A visitor who is passing over or through a country en route to some other destination. Unlike destination tourist, he spends limited time and visits few places of tourist interest.

VISITOR

Any person visiting a country other than that in which he has his usual place of residence, for any reason other than following an occupation remunerated from within the country visited.

VISUAL FLIGHT RULES (VFR)

The set of rules concerning aircraft flight where the pilot is primarily or exclusively responsible for the observation and avoidance of obstacles.

VMS, ADMINISTERED

A vertical marketing system that coordinates successive stages of production and distribution, not through common ownership or contractual ties, but through the size and power of one of the parties.

VOICE RECORDERS, COCKPIT (CVRS)

Devices which record conversations and sounds throughout an aircraft's cockpit on digital tape or on a digital microchip.

VOID

Act of invalidating a Standard Traffic Document, or coupons thereof, to prevent further use or acceptance by other carriers. The letters "VOID" must be printed between two diagonal lines across the face of the relevant coupons whenever the whole ticket is being invalidated. Otherwise, this is shown only in the "Good for Passage" box of the coupon affected including another "VOID" on the corresponding 'Reservations' area.

VOUCHER, EXCHANGE

A document issued by a carrier or its agents requesting issue of an appropriate passenger ticket and baggage check or provision of services to the person name in such document.

VOUCHERS

Documents issued by the tour operators in exchange for which travellers receive pre-paid accommodation meals, sightseeing trips etc. Also referred to as coupons.

SECTION 9: W, X, Y & Z

World tourism organization, world travel and tourism council, wholesaler, tourism promotion, world heritage site, world economic forum, worldwide fund for nature, warsaw convention, youth tourism and miscellaneous.

WAITLIST

Passengers awaiting confirmation of a request flight(s), that is/are currently fully booked.

WALKING

Sending the guest to another property when the hotel is fully occupied.

WATER SKIING

A sport practiced by being towed behind a motorboat or any large water body.

WATERFALL

A dramatic cascade of water, usually found along rivers.

WEATHER

An immediate and current set of climatic conditions such as temperature, precipitation, at mospheric pressure, winds, humidity and the percentage of clouds and sunshine.

WEB SITE/ WEB PAGE

An HTML document on the www.

WESTERN STYLE

Beds are off the floor and visible all the time.

WHITE WATER KAYAKING

Kayak is a small white boat which was earlier used by the Eskimos for seal hunting. It is highly maneuverable boat and being smaller can generally accommodate only one person.

WHITE WATER RAFTING

An inflated raft made of synthetic material to negotiate fast flowing rivers. The colour of the water turns snow white as a result of water's striking with rocks.

WHOLESALER

A supplier who sells packages through travel agents. A firm primarily engaged in wholesaling activity.

WHOLESALING

All activities involved in selling goods and services to those buying for resale or business use.

WILDLIFE SANCTUARY

In a wildlife sanctuary, protection is only given to the fauna and operations like harvesting of timber, collection of minor forest products and private ownership rights are permitted so long as they do not interfere with the well being of the animals.

WIND SURFING

A small surfboard with an attached sails used for sliding the surf on the sea. Directional control is achieved by shifting the sail position and body weight of the wind surfs.

WINE TOURISM

It involves travel undertaken for tasting, consumption or purchase of wine often at or near the source.It includes travel to the destinations /regions around the world which produce wine and include visits to wineries, wine festivals, wine tours visit to vineyards and to restaurants which offer unique vintage wines.

WINGS

The parts of an airplane that extend outward from each side of the body of the plane, called the fuselage. A wing has a curved top and a nearly flat bottom. This shape helps create the lift that raises an airplane off the ground and keeps it in the air. Wings are usually metal and cantilever (i.e., attached only at one end), completely supported by the fuselage.

WORD OF MOUTH PUBLICITY

Personal communication about a product between target buyers and neighbours, friends, family members and associates.

WORLD ECONOMIC FORUM (W E F)

The World Economic Forum (WEF) is a global community of business, political, intellectual and other leaders of society sharing the common objective of improving the state of the world. The forum is an independent, not for profit organization that brings together global leaders to work on projects that improve lives. It is headquartered on the outskirts of Geneva in a town called Cologny and has an affiliate office in New York. The participation in the WEF Summit is strictly on invitation sent by the organisers

WORLD HEALTH ORGANIZATION (WHO)

It is the United Nations specialized agency for health. It was established on 7th April 1948. WHO's objective, as set out on its constitution, is the attainment by all peoples of the highest possible level of health. WHO's Constitution as a state of complete physical, mental and social well-being and not merely the absence of disease or infirmity.

WHO is governed by 192 Members States through the World Health Assembly. The Health Assembly is composed of representatives from WHO's Member States. The main task of the World Health Assembly are to approve the WHO programme and the budget for the following biennium and to decide major policy questions.

WORLD HERITAGE SITE

A UNESCO World Heritage Site is a site (such as a forest, mountain, lake, desert, monument, building, complex, or city) that is on the list is maintained by the international World Heritage Programme administered by the UNESCO World Heritage Committee, composed of 21 state parties which are elected by their General Assembly for a four-year term. A World Heritage Site is a place of either cultural or physical significance.

The programme catalogues, names, and conserves sites of outstanding cultural or natural importance to the common heritage of humanity. Under certain conditions, listed sites can obtain funds from the World Heritage Fund. The programme was founded with the Convention Concerning the Protection of World Cultural and Natural Heritage, which was adopted by the General Conference of UNESCO on November 16, 1972. Since then, 186 state parties have ratified the convention.

As of 2009, 890 sites are listed: 689 cultural, 176 natural, and 25 mixed properties, in 148 states. Italy is home to the greatest number of World Heritage Sites to date with 44 sites inscribed on the list. UNESCO references each World Heritage Site with an identification number; but new inscriptions often include previous sites now listed as part of larger descriptions. As a result, the identification numbers exceed 1200 even though there are fewer on the list.

Each World Heritage Site is the property of the state on whose territory the site is located, but it is considered in the interest of the international community to preserve each site.

WORLD TOURISM ORGANIZATION (UNWTO)

A specialized agency of the United Nations is the leading international organization in the field of tourism. It serves as a global forum for tourism policy issues and practical source of tourism know-how.

The World Tourism Organization (UNWTO), based in Madrid, Spain, is a United Nations agency dealing with questions relating to tourism. It compiles the World Tourism rankings. The World Tourism Organization is a significant global body, concerned with the collection and collation of statistical information on international tourism. This organization represents public sector tourism bodies, from most countries in the world and the publication of its data makes possible comparisons of the flow and growth of tourism on a global scale. The official languages of UNWTO are Arabic, English, French and Russian.

The World Tourism Organization plays a role in promoting the development of responsible, sustainable and universally accessible tourism, paying particular attention to the interests of developing countries.

The Organization encourages the implementation of the Global Code of Ethics for Tourism, with a view to ensuring that member countries, tourist destinations and businesses maximize the positive economic, social and cultural effects of tourism and fully reap its benefits, while minimizing its negative social and environmental impacts.

WORLD TRAVEL AND TOURISM COUNCIL (WTTC)

It is the forum for global business leaders compromising the presidents, chairs and CEOs of 100 of the world's foremost companies. It is the only body representing the private sector in all parts of the Travel & Tourism industry worldwide.

WTTC's mission is to raise awareness of the full economic impact of the world's largest generator of wealth and jobs – Travel & Tourism. Governments are encouraged to unlock the industry's potential by adopting the Council's policy framework for sustainable tourism development.

WORLD WIDE FUND FOR NATURE (WWF)

The World Wide Fund for Nature (WWF) is an international non-governmental organization working on issues regarding the conservation, research and restoration of the environment, formerly named the World Wildlife Fund, which remains its official name in the United States and Canada. It is the world's largest independent conservation organization with over 5 million supporters worldwide, working in more than 90 countries, supporting around 1300 conservation and environmental projects around the world. It is a charity, with approximately 60% of its funding coming from voluntary donations by private individuals. 45% of the fund's income comes from the United States, the United Kingdom, and the Netherlands.

The group says its mission is "to halt and reverse the destruction of our environment". Currently, much of its work focuses on the conservation of three biomes that contain most of the world's biodiversity: forests, freshwater ecosystems, and oceans and coasts. Among other issues, it is also concerned with endangered species, pollution and climate change.

The organization was formed as a charitable trust on September 11, 1961, in Morges, Switzerland, under the name World Wildlife Fund. It was an initiative of Julian Huxley and Max Nicholson, who had thirty years experience of linking progressive intellectuals with big business interests through the Political and Economic Planning think tank.

WORLD WIDE WEB

The World Wide Web is part of the Internet and is development that has occurred to enable the easy access to information on the Internet.

WARD ROOM

Officer's recreation area where standards of appearance and conduct are relaxed

YAW

The movement of the plane as its nose turns left or right.

YIELD MANAGEMENT

A pricing method using price as a means of matching capacity with demand. The goal of yield management is to optimize the yield or contribution margin.

YIELD

Average revenue received for carrying one passenger one kilometer. To calculate yield for a given flight, divide passenger revenue for that flight by total Revenue Passenger Kilometres (RPKs).

YOUTH HOSTEL

A building which offers clean, simple and inexpensive shelter to young people exploring their own country or the world travelling independently or in a groups for holiday or educational purpose.

YOUTH TOURISM

A desire of young people to travel, which can be realized on a very large scale due to technical facilities and increase in standard of living in the wake of socialization and democratization.

YOU'RE WELCOME!

A return gesture/salutation to a person who has acknowledged you with a thank you.

Z

ZONING

Zoning is the process of applying different management objectives and regulations to different parts or zones of a specific area.It is a important tool in the site planning and design process.